SPIRITUAL FORMATION

Following the Movements of the Spirit

HENRI J. M. NOUWEN
WITH MICHAEL J. CHRISTENSEN
AND REBECCA J. LAIRD

HarperOne
An Imprint of HarperCollinsPublishers

HarperOne

FIRST EDITION

Library of Congress Cataloging-in-Publication Data
Nouwen, Henri J. M.
Spiritual formation : following the movements of the spirit / by Henri J. M.
Nouwen ; with Michael J. Christensen and Rebecca J. Laird. — 1st ed.
p. cm.
ISBN 978–0–06–168612–2
1. Spiritual life—Christianity. 2. Spiritual formation.
I. Christensen, Michael J. II. Laird, Rebecca. III. Title.
BV4501.3.N6775   2010
253.5—dc22   2010014747

10 11 12 13 14 RRD(H) 10 9 8 7 6 5 4 3 2 1

Contents

Acknowledgments

Henri Nouwen was a generous man. He gave freely of his time, money, and friendship. He wrote notes, sent gifts, and found many ways to celebrate the lives of others. It is no wonder, then, that so many of his family members and friends continue to share this characteristic openhandedness. This book would not have been possible without the collective knowledge of Henri's corpus offered by Gabrielle Earnshaw and the staff at the Henri Nouwen Archives at St. Michael's University in Toronto, who knew how to put their hands on the articles, lectures, sermons, and excerpts we requested.

Robert Jonas shared several long, leisurely conversations with us both and was a dialogue partner when we were trying to get our heads around Henri's pedagogical and theoretical interest in spiritual formation. John Mogabgab, Jim Forest, and Michael Hryniuk listened, mulled, and improved our grasp, too. Sue Mosteller and the members of the Nouwen Legacy Trust, when they evaluated and approved our proposal, and confirmed our feeling that Henri was, consciously or unconsciously, reworking the classical spiritual tradition in his approach to spiritual formation.

Kathy Smith and Maureen Wright of the Legacy Trust staff offered invaluable help with tracking down sources. To them and to the Nouwen Estate we owe an immense debt of gratitude.

Christine M. Anderson offered friendship of a rare kind and pitched in with formidable editorial skill to help sort out permissions when our time and organizational skills ran short. Our editor, Roger Freet, put up with our persistent desires to add images, have input on the cover, and fiddle endlessly with the details. Thankfully, Christina Bailly (assistant editor and art research), Carl Walesa (copy editor), and Lisa Zuniga and Carolyn Holland (production editors), of the HarperOne staff, kept us all focused on readability, clarity, aesthetics, and the production schedule.

Lastly, we are so grateful to Henri's family, especially his brother, Laurent, who embodies the Nouwen family's love of art, music, and culture. Laurent hosted us in Holland for a week of extraordinary Dutch hospitality, conversation, and laughter that helped us better understand Henri's own formation and imperfect search for intimacy with God and others. We wish to dedicate this book to Laurent, the younger brother, whose activist spirituality and practical wisdom keeps him giving to many when there is no fanfare. While Henri, the older brother, would ruminate long and hard about his spiritual insights, you, Laurent, show how to just *get out there and do it.*

PREFACE

What This Book Is About

This book is a primer on how to live a spiritual life. Rather than being about steps to enlightenment, this book is about the practices of the heart. Instead of progressive stages of development, it is about *movements*—from the things that enslave and destroy to liberation and life. This book identifies the psychospiritual dynamics, contradictions, and movements common to many who seek to live spiritually in a world of constant change and motion. This book offers spiritual wisdom on how to move from the mind to the heart and live there in the center—the place where God dwells.

"Spiritual formation presents opportunities to enter into the center of our heart and become familiar with the complexities of our own inner life," wrote Henri Nouwen, one of the most widely read and articulate spiritual writers of the late twentieth century. Beyond his forty-plus published books on Christian spirituality, this particular book contains his integrated teachings and personal examples of the "way of the heart"—the way to descend from the mind into the heart and there be shaped by the Spirit of God within. As a pastor, psychologist, professor, and pioneer in the field of pastoral psychology, Henri Nouwen is a trustworthy guide to what is now commonly called *spiritual formation*.

As a Roman Catholic, Nouwen inherited a rich tradition of spiritual formation within Catholic mystical theology that was understood as following progressive stages and applying discrete disciplines leading to spiritual union. Later, as a psychologist, he integrated and developed a more psychodynamic understanding of the inner polarities of the human psyche (soul), which he located in the heart—a person's core self or spiritual center, where one's physical, mental, and emotional lives come together as *one* in relation to God. As these inner polarities are better understood and oriented toward God, transformative movement is possible. When the human heart is open and responsive to the movements of the Spirit, healthy spiritual formation inevitably occurs.[1]

By reflecting on his own spiritual experience and the experiences of others, Nouwen was able to articulate personal and universal qualities of the inner life in relation to spiritual formation. In his first book, *Intimacy: Essays in Pastoral Psychology*, he focused on the inner dynamics of fear, shame, vulnerability, identity, self-respect, anxiety, love, and hope. These psychological and spiritual polarities, he believed, prompt transformative movements within the spiritual journey. By identifying a particular quality of inner life, he was able to articulate a corresponding discipline and movement in spiritual development—from *this* quality to *that*, from something enslaving and destructive to something liberating and life giving. For example, in his book *Reaching Out*, the first movement Nouwen identifies is *from loneliness to solitude*, requiring the discipline of silence; the second is *from hostility to hospitality*, inviting the discipline of ministry; the third movement is *from life's illusion to the prayer of the heart*, requiring both contemplative prayer and community discernment.

The movements of the Spirit—some major, some minor— may vary with the individual and with one's season of life and community of faith; they are never static, absolute, or perfectly completed, as if we must graduate from one movement to another before continuing our journey. Rather, we remain in motion and in the process of discerning which way the wind of God's activity is blowing in our lives.

To live spiritually, then, we seek to breathe with the Spirit's rhythm and move in a God-ward direction on the long walk of faith. The process involves becoming aware, naming the condition, and following the subtle movements of Spirit in our hearts and in our lives. The major movements, according to Nouwen, are *from opaqueness to transparency, from illusion to prayer, from sorrow to joy, from resentment to gratitude, from fear to love, from exclusion to inclusion,* and *from denying to befriending death.* These seven movements and many more constitute the way of the heart, the way of spiritual formation.

Spiritual Formation: Following the Movements of the Spirit is Nouwen's consolidation of the classical disciplines, traditional stages, and spiritual movements as a dynamic journey of faith requiring daily reflection and intentional practice. As such, it is suitable for individual reflection as well as small-group process.

How This Book Came to Be Written

Following the warm reception and productive feedback from *Spiritual Direction*—the earlier book we developed from Henri Nouwen's notes and manuscripts, we wondered if there might be another good book to develop from his multitude of tapes and writings. As a student of Henri's at Yale and a reader of his books since the early 1980s, I, Michael, noticed the persistent pattern of movements in his oral presentations and writings. Upon rereading his many books in later years, I started to count the number of movements he identified, noticed how he changed the names of the movements from book to book, and wondered whether this was a rhetorical or pedagogical device for easier learning, or whether the movement language was meant to describe the way God works in our hearts, moving us from one condition to another in repetitive patterns and cycles.

When my coeditor, Rebecca Laird, reexamined his psychological theory of spiritual development from his research days at the Menninger Institute and reread *The Wounded Healer*, his most important contribution to the field of pastoral psychology, it all became quite clear: Henri was reconstructing and integrating the classical stages and disciplines in light of pastoral psychology and new understandings of Christian spirituality in order to better reflect human reality in the late twentieth century. The fruit of his creative work is a new, transformative approach to spiritual formation.

This posthumous book is a product gleaned from many of Nouwen's works. Henri wrote constantly about the inner movements on his journey of faith. In the aftermath of his death, we spent a couple of years locating and pulling together various strands of his teachings about these movements in his unpublished homilies, interviews, class lecture notes, speeches, and published journal articles and books. Then we integrated them into a coherent whole in the service of new contexts and readership. Thus, movements familiar to longtime Nouwen readers are updated, restructured, and recontextualized for new audiences.

Spiritual Formation: Following the Movements of the Spirit is the second in an anticipated three-volume set on living a spiritual life. The first volume, *Spiritual Direction*, on living the questions, was published in 2006. The third, *Spiritual Discernment*, on reading the signs of daily life, is next. Each volume stands alone and can be read without having read the others. Yet together they constitute a spiritual trilogy by Henri Nouwen.[2]

How This Book Can Be Read

Formation takes time, a lifetime. This book is best ready slowly, and not necessarily sequentially, rather than all at once. Spiritual formation is personal and inward, but it is best done in a community of support. Therefore, it would be good to read this book with a small group over a period of seven weeks or even multiple months, allowing sacred time for each chapter to guide your inner work. Others who are committed to their own spiritual journey can offer support and a form of spiritual guidance along the way.

Each chapter is framed in a favorite "Henri story" or parable and a favorite "Henri icon" or image. Reading the parables out loud allows for the ancient practice of *lectio divina,* or meditative reading of sacred scripture or revelatory texts, and can lead to prayer and contemplation. The chosen images in the center section correspond to each chapter and are included because Henri often prayed with icons, taking a cue from the Orthodox Christian tradition, but also because sacred art, particularly icons, can be a source of divine revelation that the viewer is invited to receive in a meditative way in order to gain inspiration and insight. The ancient practice of meditating on visual images has recently been identified as *visio divina* (divine or sacred seeing).[3] In our world of many words, sitting in silent reflection with an image may aid in the descent of your mind into the heart. After reading a particular chapter, just sit with the corresponding image for at least ten minutes and let your mind focus on the many details in the image. Know that looking at divine images—whether religious paintings or sacred icons—is a way of seeing and a way of letting ourselves be seen. Thus image and word, looking and reflecting, are offered to help sense and tend to the movement described in each chapter.

The reflection questions in the "Going Deeper" section at the end of each chapter are meant to help you journal and apply the material in the chapter as heart knowledge that helps you better articulate the movements of your own heart and the sculpting work God is doing in your own life. The spiritual exercises included either were used by Henri Nouwen in small groups or have been added as complementary material.

If you are studying the book in a group, each session might begin with an opening prayer and ten minutes of silent *visio divina*. The images for each chapter are readily available on the Internet and could be printed out, or better yet projected on a larger screen or blank wall, for group meditation and reflection. This shared way to practice your faith together would then be followed by a discussion of three or four of the chapter's main points or quotes worth pondering. Finally, a period of sharing from the reflection questions or other exercises would follow. To honor the time commitments of the group, individuals would need to come prepared to share and willing to limit what they share to a few minutes per person to allow for all to participate. Formation in community takes discipline to let all voices be heard and not silenced or sidelined by the more extroverted members. Make sure to allow for some time to pray for each other and for the concerns of the greater world at the conclusion.

It would be a good practice, too, to end your book study with some kind of service to others beyond your group; this is a reminder that although spiritual formation has inward movements, we are always formed in the place of the heart for an encounter with God in community, expressed by love for others in ministry.

Henri Nouwen's introduction to this book—the key text for understanding his unique approach to spiritual formation—and the chapters that follow trace the inner movements and polarities of the heart in motion. Each chapter names a condition of the human experience—*opaqueness, illusion, sorrow, resentment, fear, exclusiveness, denial*—and articulates the call to prayer and spiritual formation. By following the inner movements of the Spirit, we are led, again and again, to the place of the heart where we can become formed, reformed, and transformed by God's love.

Michael J. Christensen
Rebecca J. Laird
Easter Sunday
April 4, 2010

INTRODUCTION
Spiritual Formation: The Way of the Heart

After many years of seeking to live a spiritual life, I still ask myself, "Where am I as a Christian?"—"How far have I advanced?"—"Do I love God more now than earlier in my life?"—"Have I matured in faith since I started on the spiritual path?" Honestly, I don't know the answers to these questions. There are just as many reasons for pessimism as for optimism. Many of the real struggles of twenty or forty years ago are still very much with me. I am still searching for inner peace, for creative relationships with others, and for a deeper experience of God. And I have no way of knowing if the small psychological and spiritual changes during the past decades have made me more or less a spiritual person.

In a society that overvalues progress, development, and personal achievement, the spiritual life becomes quite easily performance oriented: "On what level am I now, and how do I move to the next one?"—"When will I reach union with God?"—"When will I experience illumination or enlightenment?" Many great saints have described their religious experiences, and many lesser saints have systematized them into different phases, levels, or stages. These distinctions may be helpful for those who write books for instruction, but it is of great importance that we leave the world of measurements behind when we speak about the life of the Spirit.

Spiritual formation, I have come to believe, is not about steps or stages on the way to perfection. It's about the *movements* from the mind to the heart through prayer in its many forms that re-unite us with God, each other, and our truest selves.

The Russian mystic Theophan the Recluse wrote:

I will remind you of only one thing: one must descend with the mind into the heart, and there stand before the face of the Lord, ever-present, all seeing within you. Prayer takes a firm and steadfast hold, when a small fire begins to burn in the heart. Try not to quench this fire, and it will become established in such a way that the prayer repeats itself: and then you will have within you a small murmuring stream.[1]

All through the centuries, this view of prayer has been central in the spiritual traditions. Prayer is standing in the presence of God with the mind in the heart—that is, in the point of our being where there are no divisions or distinctions and where we are totally one within ourselves, with God, and with others and the whole of creation. In the heart of God the Spirit dwells, and there the great encounter takes place. There, heart speaks to heart as we stand before the face of the Lord, ever present, all seeing, within us. And there, in the place of the heart, spiritual formation takes place.

FORMATION OF THE HEART

The word *heart* is used here in its full biblical meaning of that place where body, soul, and spirit come together as one. In our modern milieu *heart* has become a soft word. It might refer to just feelings or the seat of the sentimental life. We think of the heart as the warm place where our emotions are located, in contrast to the cool intellect, where our thoughts find their home. But the word *heart* in Jewish-Christian tradition refers to the source of all physical, emotional, intellectual, volitional, and moral energies. It is the seat of the will; it makes plans and comes to good decisions. Thus the heart is the central unifying organ of our personal life. Our heart determines our personality, and the place where God dwells, but also the place to which the Evil One directs fierce attacks, causing us to doubt, fear, despair, resent, overconsume, and so on. Thus to live the spiritual life and to let God's presence fill us takes constant prayer, and to move from our illusions and isolation back to that place in the heart where God continues to form us in the likeness of Christ takes time and attention.

I like the following story of the sculptor, which expresses in a simple but powerful way the importance of ongoing spiritual formation:

A little boy was watching a sculptor at work. For weeks this sculptor kept chipping away at a big block of marble. After a few weeks he had created a beautiful marble lion. The little boy was amazed and said: "Mister, how did you know there was a lion in the rock?"[2]

Long before he forms the marble, the sculptor must know the lion. The sculptor must know the lion "by heart" to see him in the rock. The secret of the sculptor is that what he knows by heart he can recognize in the marble. A sculptor who knows an angel by heart will see an angel in the marble; when the sculptor knows God by heart he will see God in the marble. The sculptor certainly has to know the trade, because without skills and techniques the marble will not reveal the knowledge of the heart. But skills and techniques won't suffice unless the heart is formed by the right knowledge. The great question for the sculptor is, What do you know by heart?

The story of the boy and the sculptor helps us to see spiritual formation as formation of the heart. What is the value of well-trained and well-informed Christians and spiritual leaders when their hearts remain ignorant? What is the value of great theological erudition or great pastoral adeptness or intense but fleeting mystical experience or social activism when there is not a well-formed heart to guide a well-formed life?

Whether the knowledge of the mind leads to God or to despair depends on the heart. When the word of God remains a subject of analysis and discussion and does not descend into the heart, it can easily become an instrument of destruction instead of a guide to love. When our heart knows only evil or selfish thoughts it will evoke evil and selfishness, but when our heart is formed by the living word of God in Christ it will discern the face of God in all it sees. Theophan the Recluse also wrote:

> When remembrance of God lives in the heart and there maintains the fear of Him, then all goes well; but when this remembrance grows weak or is kept only in the head, then all goes astray.[3]

When only our mind "sees" and our heart remains blind, we remain spiritually ignorant. Therefore, spiritual formation calls for the ongoing discipline of descending from the mind into the heart so real knowledge and wisdom can be found.

THE INWARD JOURNEY TO THE HEART

Spiritual formation requires taking an inward journey to the heart. Although this journey takes place in community and leads to service, the first task in to look within, reflect on our daily life, and seek God and God's activity right there. People who dare to look inward are faced with a new and often dramatic challenge: they must come to terms with the inner *mysterium tremendum*— the overwhelming nature of the inner life.[4] Since the God "out there" or "up there" gets dissolved into the many social structures and theological constructions, the God within asks attention with a powerful force. And just as the God outside ourselves can be experienced not only as good and loving but as wrathful and demonic, the God within can be not only a creative source of a new life but also the destructive cause of chaos and confusion. That's why the greatest complaint of the mystics, like Teresa of Ávila and John of the Cross, was that they lacked spiritual guides to lead them along the right paths and enable them to distinguish between creative and destructive spirits. We hardly need to emphasize how dangerous experimentation with the interior life can be. Drugs as well as different concentration practices and withdrawal into the self often do more harm than good. On the other hand, it is becoming obvious that those who avoid the painful encounter with the unseen are doomed to live supercilious, boring, and superficial lives.

The first and most basic task of the one who takes the inward journey of the heart is to clarify the immense confusion that can arise when people enter into this new internal world. It is painful indeed to realize how poorly prepared we may be to walk this inner terrain. Most Christian leaders are used to thinking in terms of large-scale organization: getting people together in congregations, schools, and hospitals, and running the show as a circus director. They have become unfamiliar with, and even somewhat afraid of, the deep and significant movements of the

Spirit within. I am afraid that in a few decades the Church will be accused of having failed at its most basic task: to offer people creative ways to communicate with the divine source of human life.

But how can we avoid this danger? I think by no other way than to enter the heart, the center of our existence, and become familiar with the complexities of our inner lives. As soon as we feel at home in our own house—discover the dark corners as well as the light spots, the closed doors as well as the drafty rooms— our confusion will evaporate, our anxiety will diminish, and we will become capable of creative work and a spiritually informed life.

The key work here is articulation. People who can identify and articulate the movements of their inner lives, who can give names to their varied experiences, need no longer be victims of themselves but are able slowly and consistently to remove the obstacles that prevent the Spirit from entering. They can create space for the One whose heart is greater than theirs, whose eyes see more than theirs, and whose hands can heal and form more than theirs.[5]

OUR RELATIONSHIP WITH GOD

What about the most central of all relationships—our relationship with God? Can that ultimate, unseen, and unproven reality be a source of guidance and formation? Is God really present and interested in the outcome of my individual life? That is the question many people are asking today, as they have through the centuries. Today many churches, seminaries, and theological schools are beginning to understand that spiritual formation is an essential part of their educational program. For many, spirituality has seemed too personal, too private, and too elusive to be considered a serious area of study and training. Yet it might well be that, like clinical pastoral education in the 1950s and '60s, spiritual formation and spiritual direction are necessary correctives in theological education and formation in our new century.

Anyone who takes the spiritual life seriously and wants to enter more deeply into the encounter with God realizes immediately the need for formation and direction. Taking this inward journey demands looking at the movements of the heart with all its polarities, but taken in a time- and tradition-honored way. Just as we wouldn't set out on a long physical journey without planning for periods of rest and refreshment and checking our maps and directions, we can't expect to be formed in faith without committing to living a spiritual life with regular spiritual disciplines or practices.

Prayer and meditation—the central ways to develop the spiritual life—cannot be left to free-floating experimentation. The many new movements of our days are ample proof of how dangerous undirected experimentation with spiritual powers can be. When there is no one to help distinguish between the Spirit of God and the many ungodly spirits that haunt our souls, entering this precarious area might do more harm than good.

Although many people will agree with the need for spiritual formation, the question of its actual application remains for most people very difficult to answer. It is clear from the numerous "schools" in the history of Western Christian spirituality—schools represented by figures such as Pseudo-Dionysius the Areopagite, Benedict of Nursia, Francis of Assisi, Meister Eckhart, Teresa of Ávila, Ignatius of Loyola, John Wesley, George Fox, Thomas Merton, and Brother Roger and the Brothers of Taizé—that there are many methods of spiritual formation. But it is possible to discover, underneath this great variety, a few practices that can be isolated as guides for all those who are concerned with their own and other people's spiritual growth. I will focus here on five practices that seem of special importance: *reflection* on the living documents of our own hearts and times, *lectio divina, silence, com-*

munity, and *service.* Practiced together, especially with a spiritual director and community of faith, these areas of discipline help fashion our hearts for God.

REFLECTION ON OUR OWN HEARTS AND TIMES

The authentic spiritual life finds its basis in the human condition. The spiritual life is not lived outside, before, after, or beyond our everyday existence. No, the spiritual life can be real only as it is lived in the midst of the pains and joys of the here and now. Therefore, we need to begin with a careful look at the way we think, speak, feel, and act from hour to hour, day to day, week to week, and year to year, in order to become more fully aware of our hunger for the Spirit. As long as we have only a vague inner feeling of discontent with our present way of living, and only an indefinite desire for "things spiritual," our lives will continue to stagnate in a generalized melancholy. We often say, "I am not very happy. I am not content with the way my life is going. I am not really joyful or peaceful. But I don't know how things can be different, and I guess I have to be realistic and accept my life as it is." It is this mood of resignation that prevents us from actively naming our reality, articulating our experience, and moving more deeply into the life of the Spirit.

In my own training at the Menninger Clinic in the late 1960s, I studied and wrote about the life and thought of Anton T. Boisen, one of the pioneers in the psychology of religion and the modern pastoral-care movement. Boisen's work is intensely autobiographical. His own call to the ministry was followed by "years of wandering" that became intensified during a period of mental disturbance in which he began to "read" the document of his own life. Boisen felt that studying the spiritual life with God "must not begin with tradition or systems formulated in books, but with open minded exploration of living human experience."[6]

Actively reflecting on what Boisen called "the living document" of your life and times clarifies the inner polarities of our human condition and points toward a greater wholeness. In gaining knowledge of the heart, we find that "what is most personal is most universal."[7]

LECTIO DIVINA

The term *lectio divina* comes from the Benedictine tradition and refers primarily to the sacred or devotional reading of the Bible.[8] My growing suspicion is that our competitive, productive, skeptical, and sophisticated society inhibits our reading and being read by the Word of God. *Lectio divina* means to read the Bible with reverence and openness to what the Spirit is saying to us in the present moment. When we approach the Word of God as a word spoken to me, God's presence and will can be made known. The regular practice of *lectio divina* presents occasions when my story and God's story meet, and in that moment something surprising can happen. To read the Bible in this way means therefore to read "on my knees"—reverently, attentively, and with the deep faith that God has a word for me in my own unique situation.

The Bible is primarily a book not of information but of formation, not merely a book to be analyzed, scrutinized, and discussed but a sacred book to nurture us, to unify our hearts and minds, and to serve as a constant source of contemplation. It is important to guard against the temptation to read the Bible programmatically as a book full of good stories and telling illustrations that can help us with instant advice, sermons, lectures, papers, and articles. As long as we deal with the Word of God as an instrument with which we can do many useful things, we don't really read the Bible. The Bible does not speak to us as long as we want only to use it. But when we are willing to hear the Word as a word for us, sacred scripture can disclose itself, and its message can penetrate into the center of our hearts. This is far from easy, because it requires openness and the constant willingness to be converted, and to be led to places where we would rather not go (John 21:18).

When St. Augustine read the Bible prayerfully and received the Word meditatively as a word spoken directly to him, his life changed radically. Other saints in history and many people today tell the same story of spiritual transformation. Conversion and transformation by the Word of God always opens us to the Spirit of truth and helps us break through the paralyzing ignorance of our worldly life. *Lectio divina* is an ancient practice of spiritual formation that we still need today.

As our society becomes less word oriented and more visually focused, other methods of receiving God's word are needed. *Sacred looking,*[9] or divine gazing at icons and religious images, is reemerging as a new way to see and sense the movement of God in our lives. In earlier centuries Orthodox Christians painted and prayed with icons, knowing that these objects could lead them to the inner room of prayer and bring them closer to the heart of God. Personally, I know the power of prayer while gazing upon an icon. There have been many times when I could not pray, when I was too tired to read the gospels, too restless to have spiritual thoughts, too depressed to find words for God, or too exhausted to do anything; but I found that I could still look at images that were able to immediately and intimately connect me with an experience of God's love. I learned to take a copy of Rublev's icon of the Holy Trinity and a print of van Gogh's *Sunflowers* with me when traveling. Even in the most distracting and despairing of times, these sacred images are windows into the heart of God.[10]

SILENCE

Without silence the Word of God cannot bear fruit. One of the most depressing aspects of contemporary life is the almost complete absence of silence. I wonder if the Word of God can really be received in the center of our hearts if our constant chatter and noise and electronic interactions keep blocking the way of the heart. As Ambrose of Milan says, "By silence have I seen many saved, by words none." And as Saint Seraphim of Sarov says: "Silence is the sacrament of the world to come, words are the weapons of this world."[11]

The mystics all agree that silence is the royal road to spiritual formation. I have never met anyone seriously interested in the spiritual life who did not have a growing desire for silence. Those who search for the Spirit of truth become more and more aware that "among all the parts of the body, the tongue is a whole wicked world in itself" (James 3:6). As long as our hearts and minds are filled with words of our own making, there is no space for the Word to enter deeply into our hearts and bear fruit. In and through silence the Word of God descends from the mind into the heart, where we can ruminate on it, masticate it, digest it, and let it become flesh and blood in us. This is the meaning of *meditation*. Without silence the Word cannot become our inner guide; without meditation it cannot build its home in our hearts and speak from there.

The royal road to the heart by way of the Word in silence is not an easy discipline. We often get distracted and confused: we do not know which inner experiences to trust and which to mistrust, which promptings to follow and which to avoid. The descent from the mind into the heart, which is the way of spiritual formation, is not without pitfalls. Therefore, it is not surprising that those who take the spiritual life seriously are always seeking guidance. One of the most encouraging signs in recent years is the development of centers where people are trained in spiritual direction. There is a growing search for inner freedom and a growing need for people who can help in the task of discernment—distinguishing the Holy Spirit from the many unholy spirits. This is when spiritual direction can be especially helpful.

Lectio divina, silence, discernment, and spiritual direction are central elements in spiritual formation. Whichever particular "school of prayer" we follow, they all stress that the Word of God needs to be received in solitude and silence, under the eye of a competent guide. This is not the final word on spiritual formation; in fact, it could even be misleading, since it might suggest that spiritual formation is a highly individual affair. I read the Word alone. I enter into silence and solitude. I may talk with a specialist to help me walk the way of the heart. But these are not enough. Spiritual formation is not an exercise of private devotion but one of corporate spirituality. We do have personal experiences of God, but together we are formed as the people of God.

THE OUTWARD JOURNEY TO COMMUNITY

Spiritual formation requires taking not only the *inward journey* to the heart, but also the *outward journey* from the heart to community and ministry. Christian spirituality is essentially communal. Spiritual formation is formation in community. One's personal prayer life can never be understood if it is separated from community life. Prayer in the spiritual life leads to community, and community to prayer. In community we learn what it means to confess our weakness and to forgive each other. In community we discover our own woundedness, but also a place of healing. In community we learn true humility. Without community, we become individualistic and egocentric. Therefore, spiritual formation always includes formation to life in community.

Reflection on the heart, *lectio divina,* silence, discernment, and guidance can come to full fruition only in the context of a spiritual community and faith tradition. Therefore, the reading of the Word of God and the silent listening to it are not individual techniques taught by a master, practiced only in solitude, and leading to personal perfection. A spiritual director is not a guru whose authority depends on personal enlightenment, but a person of faith and a discerning companion who listens well and prays with you. I think that here we touch on the difference between Christian spirituality and many Eastern religions and methods.

Christian spirituality not only flows from community but creates community. It nurtures the life of the Spirit in us, within us, and among us. The Spirit of God dwells in the center of our heart and is the center of our life together. Indeed, what is most personal proves to be most communal; what is most intimate proves to be the most public; what is most nourishing for our individual lives proves to be the best food for our lives as the people of God living in and acting on behalf of a suffering world. It is therefore not surprising that prayer and community are always found together, because the same Spirit who prays in us is the Spirit who binds us together into one body as we are called to love each other and work for a renewed world.

Spiritual community is primarily a quality of the heart that enables us to unmask the illusions of our competitive society and look straight at reality. In and through community we come to recognize each other as brothers and sisters in Christ and sons and daughters of the same God. Because it is a quality of the heart, community cannot be identified with any particular institutional form. Community is a gift of the Spirit that may present itself in many different ways: in silence as well as in words; in listening as well as in speaking; in living together as well as in a solitary life; and in various forms of worship and active service.

SERVICE

To serve means to minister, to love and care for others, and to recognize in them the heart of God. A true disciple of Jesus will always go to where people are feeling weak, broken, sick, in pain, poor, lonely, forgotten, anxious, and lost. It is often hard to go to places of weakness and rejection to offer consolation and comfort. It is possible only when we discover the presence of Jesus among the poor and weak and realize the many gifts they have to offer. Therefore, spiritual formation always includes responding from the heart to the needs of the poor in a spirit of true compassion.

Since many of us are tempted to understand the formation of the heart in individualistic terms, it is important to remember that community leads to ministry, and ministry means service to the people of God. It can never be reduced to psychological models in which the one-to-one relationship is central. When the disciplines of the Word, silence, and guidance are practiced in an individualistic milieu, they may well do no more than nourish our narcissistic tendencies and strengthen spiritual self-centeredness.

The Word of God is first of all read in community, silence is first a part of our life together, spiritual direction first needs to be seen and experienced as direction in the name of the larger community, and ministry is a vocation given by and performed in the name of the community of faith. Thus, spiritual formation means ongoing formation of the heart, in community life, expressed in service to the world.

SPIRITUAL FORMATION: THE WAY TO FREEDOM

The best way to articulate the importance of spiritual formation today, I believe, is to see it as the way of the heart, the way to freedom. The way of the heart is from solitude with God to community with God's people to ministry to and for all. The way of the heart is the way to truth, and "the truth will make you free" (John 8:32).

When Jesus left his disciples, he said: "It is to your advantage that I go away, for if I do not go away, the Advocate will not come to you; but if I go, I will send him to you . . . he will guide you into all the truth" (John 16:7–13). The Spirit of truth liberates us from our ignorance and illusions, which keep us enslaved. Ignorance makes us look for acceptance where it cannot be expected, and makes us hope for changes where they cannot be found. Illusion makes us fight for a new world as if we could create and control it ourselves; it makes us judge our neighbors as if we had the final word. Ignorance and illusion keep us entangled in the world and cause suffering and sorrow. But the way of the heart leads to freedom.

The spiritual life is a life in which we are set free by the Spirit of God to enjoy life in all its fullness. By this Spirit we can indeed "be in the world without being of it"; we can move freely without being bound by false attachments; we can speak freely without fear of human rejection; and we can live with peace and joy even when surrounded by conflict and sadness.

It was this Spirit that set the first-century disciples free to travel great distances and boldly speak the Word of God even when it led to persecution, imprisonment, and death. It is this same Spirit that will give us the freedom to live in our death-oriented society as witnesses to new life given to us in and through Jesus Christ. Spiritual formation prepares us for a life in which we move away from our fears, compulsions, resentments, and sorrows, to serve with joy and courage in the world, even when this leads us to places we would rather not go. Spiritual formation helps us to see the face of God in the midst of a hardened world and in our own heart. This freedom helps us to use our skills and our very lives to make that face visible to all who live in bondage and fear. As Jesus told his disciples: "So, if the Son makes you free, you will be free indeed" (John 8:36).

The chapters that follow trace the inner polarities in the movements from the mind into the heart and beyond. Each chapter names a condition of the human experience—opaqueness, illusion, sorrow, resentment, fear, exclusiveness, denial—and articulates the call to prayer, movement, and spiritual formation. By following the inner movements of the spiritual life, we are led by the Spirit of God, again and again, to the place of the heart where we can be whole.

Henri Nouwen

PART ONE

Early Movements

ONE

From Opaqueness to Transparency

~ The Empty Teacup ~

There is a story about a university professor who came to a
Zen master to ask him about Zen. Nan-in, the Zen master,
served him tea. He poured his visitor's cup full, and then
kept pouring. The professor watched the overflow until he
could no longer restrain himself. "It is over-full. No more
will go in!" "Like this cup," Nan-in said, "you are full of
your own opinions and speculations. How can I teach you
Zen unless you first empty your cup?"

—*101 Zen Stories*, a 1919 compilation of Zen koans
from the Meiji era (1868–1912) in Japan[1]

Spiritual formation begins with the gradual and often painful
discovery of God's incomprehensibility in the face of life's great
mysteries and limitations. We might be competent in many
subjects, but we cannot become an expert in the things of God.
God is greater than our minds and cannot be caught within the

boundaries of our finite concepts. Thus, spiritual formation leads not to a proud understanding of divinity, but to *docta ignorantia,* an "articulate not-knowing."

GOD CANNOT BE CONTAINED

God cannot be "caught" or "comprehended" in any specific idea, concept, opinion, or conviction. God cannot be defined by any specific emotion or spiritual sensation. God cannot be identified with good feelings, right intentions, spiritual fervor, generosity of spirit, or unconditional love. All these experiences may remind us of God's presence, but their absence does not prove God's absence. God is greater than our minds and greater than our hearts, and just as we have to avoid the temptation of adapting God to our finite small concepts, we have to avoid adapting God to our limited small feelings.

This is a difficult reality to accept in a culture that suggests we are trained to master a subject, define all knowledge, and control our destinies. Doctors, lawyers, and psychologists study to become qualified professionals who are paid to know what to do. A well-trained theologian or minister is only able to point out the universal tendency to narrow God down to our own little conceptions and expectations, and to call for an open mind and heart for God to be revealed.

How then are we, like the professor in the parable, to seek this incomprehensible God? When we are willing to empty our cup and detach ourselves from making our individual experience the criterion for our approach to others, we may be able to see that life is greater than our personal life, history is greater than our family history, experience greater than our own experience, and God greater than our god.

Both theological reflection and spiritual formation require an articulate not-knowingness and a receptive emptiness through which God can be revealed. Just as theology asks us to empty our cup so that we can open our mind to the incomprehensible things of God, spirituality asks us to empty our mind so we can open our heart to receive life as a gift to be lived. Even more than our mind, it is our heart that needs to become empty enough for the Spirit to enter and fill it. This process of self-emptying and spirit filling is called *spiritual formation*—the gradual development of the heart of God in the life of a human being, aided by contemplative prayer, inclusive community, and compassionate ministry.

CONTEMPLATIVE PRAYER MAKES THE CLOUDED CLEAR

For those who pray from the heart, the world loses its *opaqueness* and becomes *transparent:* that is, the world of experience starts pointing beyond itself to the luminous Source of wisdom and understanding, to the translucent realm of the Spirit of God. To contemplate is to *see,* to make visible that which is hidden from ordinary sight.

Evagrius Ponticus, one of the Desert Fathers who had great influence on monastic spirituality in the East and the West, calls contemplation a *theoria physike,* which means a vision (*theoria*) of the real nature of things (*physike*). The contemplative is someone who *sees* things for what they really are, who sees the real connections of how things hang together, who knows—as Thomas Merton used to say—"what the scoop is." To attain such a vision, spiritual discipline is necessary. Evagrius calls this discipline the *praktike*—the taking away of the blindfolds that prevent us from seeing clearly. Merton, who was very familiar with Evagrius's teaching, expressed the same idea when he said that the contemplative life is a life in which we constantly move from opaqueness to transparency, from the place where things are dark, thick, impenetrable, and closed to the place where these same things are translucent, open, and offer vision far beyond themselves.[2]

The practice of contemplative prayer reveals to us the true nature of things; it unmasks the illusion of control, the possessiveness of possessions, and the pretense of the false self. For those who practice contemplative prayer, the world (*mundus*) no longer is opaque or dark but has become new and transparent—the "new earth" shining with its inherent character. To live spiritually in the world is to unmask the illusion, dispel the darkness, and walk in the light.

Just as a window is not real if we cannot look through it, so our world cannot show its true identity if it remains opaque and does not point beyond itself. In the process of spiritual formation, all of life can become a *theoria physike,* a clear vision of the nature of things. The Spirit of God shows us how to move continuously from opaqueness to transparency in three central relationships: our relationship with *nature,* with *time,* and with *people.*

How Nature Is Transformed

In recent decades we have become particularly aware of the crucial importance of our relationship with the natural environment. All of nature conceals great secrets that cannot be revealed to us if we do not listen carefully to and see spiritually its true form.

John Henry Newman views the visible world as a veil "so that all that exists or happens visibly, conceals and yet suggests, and above all serves, a greater system of persons, facts and events beyond itself."[3] How differently we would live if we were constantly aware of this veil and sensed in our whole being that nature desires us to hear and see the great story of God's love to which it points.

When we relate to the trees, the rivers, the mountains, the fields, and the oceans as objects that we can use according to our real or fabricated needs, nature is opaque and does not reveal to us its true being. When a tree is nothing but a potential chair, it ceases to tell us much about growth; when a river is only a dumping place for industrial wastes, it can no longer speak to us about movement; and when a flower is nothing more than a model for a plastic decoration, it has little to say about the simple beauty of life. Our dirty rivers, smog-filled skies, strip-mined hills, and ravaged woods are opaque signs in our society that manifest themselves as pollution and ecological disaster, revealing our false relationship with nature.

It is sad that so many do not believe in the ministry of nature to us. We easily limit ministry to the work of people for people. But we could do an immense service to our world if we would let nature heal, counsel, and teach again. Our difficult and now urgent task is to move from viewing nature as a property to own, a possession to be conquered, or an object to be used to seeing its true beauty and glory. When we grab a flower, for example, it withers in our hand. A flower is not meant to be grabbed, but patiently pondered. Then it will open up to us its true beauty. A friend once gave me a beautiful photograph of a water lily. I asked him how he had been able to take such a splendid picture. With a smile he said, "Well, I had only to be very patient and very attentive. It was only after a few hours of compliments that the lily was willing to let me take her picture."

When we contemplate creation rather than manipulating it, we are able to see nature as a gift of God to be cherished and cared for. When we receive in our hearts with gratitude and awe what God has created, we see nature as it truly is—a transcendent reality that asks for reverence and respect. Then it becomes transparent, and life starts to speak a new language, revealing to us the goodness and beauty of God. The plants and animals with whom we live teach us about birth, growth, maturation, and death, about the need for gentle care, and especially about the importance of patience and hope.

This is the sacramental basis of any healthy ecology. Bread is more than bread: it points to the One who broke bread with his friends. Water is more than water: it points to our spiritual birth. Wine is more than the fruit of the vine, made by human hands. It becomes for us the blood of Christ, the cup of salvation. Most profoundly, all the elements remembered in the Great Thanksgiving point beyond themselves to the great story or our re-creation. Food and drink, clothes and homes, mountains and rivers, oceans and skies—all become transparent when nature discloses itself to those with eyes to see the loving face of the God

How Time Is Converted

A second relationship that requires the ongoing movement from opaqueness to transparency is how we view time. In the process of spiritual formation, not only nature but the quality of time is recalibrated.

Time constantly threatens to become our enemy. Time enslaves us. We say, "I wish I could do all the things that I need to do, but I simply have no time. Just thinking about all the things I have to do today—buy groceries at the store, practice my music, finish writing a paper, show up at class, make a dozen phone calls, visit a friend, do my exercise and meditation—just thinking about these makes me tired." The most common request nowadays is: "I know how busy you are, but do you have a minute?" And the most important decisions are often made while "grabbing a bite." Indeed, it seems that we no longer have any time, but rather that time has us.

When we experience time as *chronos* (chronology), the events of our life are nothing more than a randomly connected series of incidents and accidents over which we have no control. Time has become opaque, dark, and impenetrable. We cannot *see through* to the underlying coherence of our story. Disappointments, unemployment, material loss, sickness, and death are experienced as meaningless disruptions to be denied and avoided if possible. When time is only *chronos,* we don't have time to do all the things we need to do, and our schedule is a burden. Time is running out, and life is exhausting. There is no time for friendship, for blessing, for celebration.

Time needs to be converted from *chronos* to *kairos*—an opportunity for a change of heart. The spiritual life is a formation process in which time slowly loses its opaqueness and becomes transparent. To start seeing that the many events of our day, week, or year are not obstacles to a full and meaningful life, but the way to it, is a real experience of conversion. Once we discover that writing letters, attending classes, visiting friends, cooking food, and even doing the dishes are not a series of random activities but contain within themselves the transforming power of re-creation, we move from time lived as *chronos* to time lived as *kairos* (right time, the real moment, the opportunity for change, the chance of a lifetime). When our time becomes *kairos,* endless new possibilities and opportunities open up to our vision.

In Jesus's life and ministry, every event is recognized as *kairos.* He opens his public ministry with these words: "The *time* has come . . ." (Mark 1:15). He lives each moment of life as an opportunity to make all things new. After just three and a half years, he announces that his *time* is near (Mark 26:10) and enters into his last hour. And finally, as physical death is transformed into resurrected life, Jesus liberates human history from mere chronology to *kairos*—God's time, where past, present, and future merge in the present moment.

When time is converted so that what is opaque becomes transparent, we start to recognize God's hands at work, molding the world as well as our individual lives into living reminders of God's love. Then we can proclaim the gospel: This is God's world. Time is in God's hands. Something profound is happening. History has purpose. "In all things God works for the good" (Rom. 8:28). What seem to be just chipped pieces of marble are really patterns in the mosaic of God's work in our lives. With the eyes of faith we can learn from the events of our life and can receive whatever happens as from the hand of God. Even hard and painful times can be converted to occasions for learning, shaping influences forming us into the persons we are and leading us to the Source of healing and salvation.

The spiritual life, therefore, is not a life that offers a few good moments between the many bad ones, but an abundant life that transforms all moments of time into windows through which the invisible becomes visible.

How People Are Transfigured

For those who pray, not only do nature and time lose their opaqueness, but most profoundly, *people* become increasingly transparent. Here more than in our relationships with nature and with time, the importance of contemplation as *theoria physike*—as seeing the real connections—becomes manifest.

Our society makes it difficult to see people as transparent because we are conditioned to relate to persons as characters—different, interesting or not interesting—to use as we need or want. "Oh, she is good at that, and he is good at this, so let me manipulate, exploit, or use them for their valuable function," we often think to ourselves.

One of our greatest temptations is to be selective about whom we want to relate to. When we see someone who strikes us as an "interesting" person, we want to get to know them as someone "worth" knowing for their special qualities. We are always intrigued by interesting figures in sports, entertainment, arts, and sciences. We give them our special attention and want to meet them, shake their hand, get their autograph, or just gaze upon them. We are also curious and intrigued by unusual characters: criminals, the physically handicapped, the pathologically driven, or the psychologically disturbed. Sometimes our attention is instinctively drawn to them. In the medical and helping professions, characterization is common. We generalize and label people as "sick" or "healthy," "unstable" or "stable," "addicted" or "codependent," and so forth. In religious circles, we often divide people into two camps: believers and nonbelievers, churched and unchurched, conservatives and progressives, orthodox and non-orthodox, saint and sinner. Characterization is common but narrowing. Labeling is always limiting. It reveals a lot about our own insecurities and gives us a false understanding of the real nature of our neighbors.

A teacher is more than a teacher, and computer technicians and auto mechanics are more than their functions. A person is more than his or her character or figure. If you relate to me only as someone who can do something for you or whom you can use for your own purposes, then I am not going to show my best self to you. I am going to become defensive, suspicious, a little careful, and I may hide my true feelings and opinions. But if you see in me more than my character, if you see me as a unique *person*, then I can slowly communicate to you on a deeper level, and may even share my secrets.

The word *person* comes from the Old French *per-sonare*, which means "sounding through." Our spiritual task is to resist the temptation to box our fellow human beings into figures and characters, and to see them rather as persons who "sound through" to a greater reality than they themselves fully know. As persons we sound through a love greater than we ourselves can grasp, a truth deeper than we ourselves can articulate, and a beauty richer than we ourselves can contain.

When in contemplation we come to see all of life as a gift, we then recognize the people in our lives as the greatest gifts of God. No longer characters, they have become persons with whom we can form community and through whom God can speak. When we become persons for each other, we transcend the limitations of our individual characters and realize a greater purpose as the people of God. As persons uniquely created by God, we are called to be transparent to each other, to point far beyond our character to the One who has given us true love, truth, and beauty.

Spiritual formation requires a constant discipline of prayer to move from opaqueness to transparency, a discipline by which a world of darkness is transformed into one of transcendent light. Nature no longer is a property to control but a gift to be received and shared. Time no longer is a random series of events but a constant opportunity for a change of heart. When time is converted from *chronos* to *kairos* (and from history to his-story), we can seize the present moment and be at peace. And when people are no longer interesting characters to meet or exploit for our own purpose but persons "sounding through" more than they can contain, they can be loved and protected and understood. Contemplative prayer helps us remove our blindfolds and see the world as it truly is—as *sacramental*—connected and constantly revealing to us the great love of God.

CONTEMPLATION AND MINISTRY

Contemplative prayer often brings us to an intimate encounter with the love of God, revealed to us in Jesus. In such an experience we come to know ever more deeply that God is not against us, but for us; not far from us, but with us; not outside of us, but deeply within. As we take a quiet moment to reflect in a peaceful place, our minds and hearts become still and, in this stillness, become deeper and wider, inviting/unbinding the eternal quality of life in all its fullness. It is in this growing inner awareness of the eternal embrace of God that we find our true freedom.

According to Evagrius, the practice of *theoria physike* (contemplation of the real nature of things) finds its culmination in *theologia* (direct knowledge of God). Here we go beyond the vision of the nature of things and enter into a most intimate communion with God as Holy Trinity. This *theologia* is the greatest gift of all, the grace of complete unity, rest, and peace. It is the highest level of spiritual life, in which the created world is transcended and we experience directly our being lifted up into God's inner life.[4] This mountaintop experience is given only rarely, and even those who see from on high must return to the valley, not telling anyone what they have seen (Luke 9:36). For most of us, the greater part of life is not on the mountain but in the valley. And in this valley we are called to prayer as active ministry.

When we unmask the illusions around us, those whose lives we touch are also enlightened. When the world is no longer dark and opaque to us, others begin to see the light. A person might say, "What do you see in me that I cannot see?" And you might respond: "I see great beauty coming through you. In meeting you I come in touch with a deep love and sense of awe." We are often shining through to each other the realities that we ourselves do not yet see or fully understand. Ministry is how we make the world more transparent to the other so that the world speaks of God and people are enlightened by the love of God.

There is something beautiful there, lurking beneath the surface, for those with eyes to see and ears to hear. Ministry is to help others open their eyes and ears, so to speak—to make what is cloudy and opaque clear and beautiful. What we have experienced in prayer, we proclaim to others: "You are a much more loving person than you realize. There is something more beautiful in nature than you may see. There is something more happening in your life than you might think, or be able to see right now."

Contemplation cleanses the mind and opens the heart to receive God's truth, beauty, and wisdom. The illusions of life are unmasked, and true vision is possible. Darkness is dispelled, and divine light shines through. The world loses its opaqueness and becomes transparent. Nature is transformed, time is converted, and people are transfigured. *God makes all things new.*

GOING DEEPER:
EXERCISES FOR
SPIRITUAL FORMATION

REFLECT AND JOURNAL

1. Imagine your life as a cup overfull of opinions, ideas, and activities. Make a list of the many distractions that you might want to ask God prayerfully to remove in order to make room for a wider view of your life and God's world.

2. "Those who are sensitive to the enormous ecological problem of our age and work hard to take away some of nature's opaqueness," writes Nouwen in *Clowning in Rome*, "fulfill a real ministry, because they allow not only people but also plants and animals to teach about the cycle of life, to heal the lonely, and to tell of the great love of God. Thus the movement from opaqueness to transparency in our relationship with nature not only leads to a deeper contemplation of the world that surrounds us, but also broadens our ministry in the world."[5] How might this insight transform your own ministry of caring, teaching, healing, counseling, worship, and so on?

3. Think of a time when someone else saw something in you that you simply could not see. Reflect on how that experience allowed you to expand your self-perception. How might God's view of you as "beloved" transform your life as one through whom God shines?

VISIO DIVINA: THE TRANSFIGURATION

One way to pray contemplatively is to behold the beauty of the
Lord by gazing at the Byzantine icon of the Transfiguration from
Pereslavl (c. 1403) by Theophan the Greek. (See color insert.)
This activity can be called *visio divina*. In the Gospel of Luke,
Jesus goes up to the mountain—with Peter, James, and John—to
pray. On the mountaintop, what was clouded was made clear:
"While he was praying, his face changed its appearance and his
clothes became dazzling white." The glory of God broke through
the darkness, and those who went up with him saw the light of
his divine majesty shining through the veil of his status as servant. Slowly, they began to realize that it would be their task to
"sound through" in their own personalities the words that they
had heard on the mountaintop: "This is my Son, whom I have
chosen, listen to him" (Luke 9:28–35).

The icon of the Transfiguration was created from the visionary
images in the Gospels for the sole purpose of offering access to
the inner sanctuary of prayer and brings us close to the heart of
God. Icons offer us real but limited access to the uncreated light
of God's glory and to our own spiritual illumination. Through
the gate of the visible we behold the mystery of the invisible.
Prayerfully gazing at the icon offers us a chance to "see" more
clearly into the true nature of things. As you contemplate the
image, try to see its luminous splendor, feel its majesty, enjoy its
texture of colors, study its forms and symmetry, ponder the communion of Jesus, Moses, and Elijah, and try to empathize with
the reactions of the three disciples. Then enter into the mystery
of the transformation that takes place in the presence of Jesus on
the mountain of prayer. There, high on the mountain, the familiar face of our teacher is revealed in a new light.

For those who gaze on the beauty of the Lord, what is opaque
becomes transparent; nature, time, and people are transformed;
and we ourselves are transfigured.

TWO

From Illusion to Prayer

~ The Useless Tree ~

A carpenter and his apprentice were walking together through a large forest. And when they came across a tall, huge, gnarled, old, beautiful tree, the carpenter asked his apprentice: "Do you know why this tree is so tall, so huge, so gnarled, so old and beautiful?" The apprentice looked at his master and said: "No . . . why?"

"Well," the carpenter said, "because it is useless. If it had been useful it would have been cut long ago and made into tables and chairs, but because it is useless it could grow so tall and so beautiful that you can sit in its shade and relax."

—adapted from Chuang Tzu, *The Inner Chapters*[1]

Spiritual formation is a call to discipleship, a call to follow Jesus radically and so become his true brothers and sisters—sons and daughters of God. When we belong to Jesus, we belong with him to his heavenly Father, and to each other. Having found our true home in God, we then can live in the world without becoming subject to its obsessions, compulsions, and addictions.

Discipleship, however, calls for discipline. Indeed, *discipleship* and *discipline* share the same linguistic root (from *discere*, which means "to learn from"), and the two should never be separated. Whereas discipline without discipleship leads to rigid formalism, discipleship without discipline ends in sentimental romanticism. It requires an enormous human effort to be and to stay in the world with its many demands while keeping our hearts and minds solidly anchored in God. The various disciplines of the spiritual life are meant for freedom and are reliable means for the creation of helpful boundaries in our lives within which God's voice can be heard, God's presence felt, and God's guidance experienced. Without such boundaries that make space for God, our lives quickly narrow down; we hear and see less and less, we become spiritually sick, and we become one-dimensional, and sometimes delusional, people. The only remedy for this is the intentional practice of prayer and meditation.

WHAT IS PRAYER?

The discipline of prayer is the intentional, concentrated, and regular effort to create space for God. Everything and everyone around us wants to fill up every bit of space in our lives and so make us not only occupied people, but preoccupied people as well. When we permit the world to pack our minds and hearts with countless things to look at, listen to, and read about, and countless people to visit, write to, talk to, and worry about, how do we focus? When there are countless happenings to be excited or depressed about, how can we ever manage to keep a space for the One who says: "Do not set your heart on all these things. Set your hearts on God's Kingdom first . . . and all these other things will be given you as well" (Matt. 6:33–34)?

A life without a quiet center easily becomes delusional. When we cling to the results of our actions as our only way of self-identification, we become possessive, defensive, and dependent on false identities. In the solitude of prayer we slowly unmask the illusion of our dependencies and possessiveness, and discover in the center of our own self that we are not what we can control or conquer but what is given to us from above to channel to others. In solitary prayer we become aware that our identity does not depend on what we have accomplished or possess, that our productivity does not define us, and that our worth is not the same as our usefulness.

PRAYER IS WASTING TIME WITH GOD

The world says, "If you are not making good use of your time, you are useless." Jesus says: "Come spend some useless time with me." If we think about prayer in terms of its *usefulness* to us—what prayer will do for us, what spiritual benefits we will gain, what insights we will gain, what divine presence we may feel—God cannot easily speak to us. But if we can detach ourselves from the idea of the usefulness of prayer and the results of prayer, we become free to "waste" a precious hour with God in prayer. Gradually, we may find, our "useless" time will transform us, and everything around us will be different.

Prayer is being unbusy with God instead of being busy with other things. Prayer is primarily to do nothing useful or productive in the presence of God. To not be useful is to remind myself that if anything important or fruitful happens through prayer, it is God who achieves the result. So when I go into the day, I go with the conviction that God is the one who brings forth fruit in my work, and I do not have to act as though I am in control of things. I have to work hard; I have to do my task; I have to offer my best. But I can let go of the illusion of control and be detached from the result. At the end of each day I can prayerfully say that if something good has happened, God be praised.

PRAYER IS BEING ALONE WITH GOD

Solitary prayer takes a central place in the life and ministry of Jesus. The Gospels record how often Jesus prays by himself and with others. Prayer for Jesus seems to be a daily routine:

> That evening, after sunset, they brought to him all who were sick and those who were possessed by devils. The whole town came crowding round the door, and he cured many who were suffering from diseases of one kind or another; he also cast out many devils, but he would not allow them to speak, because they knew who he was. *In the morning, long before dawn, he got up and left the house, and went off to a lonely place and prayed there.* Simon and his companions set out in search of him, and when they found him they said, "Everybody is looking for you." He answered, "Let us go elsewhere, to the neighboring country towns, so that I can preach there too, because that is why I came." And he went all through Galilee, preaching in their synagogues and casting out devils. (Mark 1:32–39; emphasis mine)

In the midst of a busy schedule of activities—healing suffering people, casting out devils, responding to impatient disciples, traveling from town to town, and preaching from synagogue to synagogue—we find these quiet words: "In the morning, long before dawn, he got up and left the house, and went off to a lonely place and prayed there." The more I read this nearly silent sentence locked in between the loud words of action, the more I have the sense that the secret of Jesus's ministry is hidden in that lonely place where he went to pray, early in the morning, long before dawn. In the center of breathless activities we hear a restful breathing. Surrounded by hours of moving we find a moment of quiet stillness. In the heart of much involvement there are words of withdrawal. In the midst of action there is contemplation. And after much togetherness there is solitude. In the lonely place Jesus finds the courage to follow God's will and not his own; to speak God's words and not his own; to do God's work and not his own. It is in the lonely place, where Jesus enters into intimacy with the Father, that his ministry is born.

In solitary prayer Jesus comes to understand his identity and mission. In prayer, he experiences God's will and direction, and affirms that it is God who sends him, who gives him the words to say and the deeds to fulfill. Jesus never claims any glory for himself but always refers to God's glory: "The words I am speaking are not my words but those given to me by my Father. The works I am doing are not my works, but the works of my Father. The glory to which I bear witness is not my glory, but the glory of my Father" (John 5:30, 14:10).

For Jesus, and for us, prayer provides the insight and affirmation that if we do anything that is worthwhile—teaching, healing, organizing, reforming, working for good—we can never claim it as our own achievement. Rather, we can acknowledge it as a gift of God, the result of which is in God's hands. Prayer is the experience of knowing that God is the source of everything we claim as our own. To pray is to say with Jesus, "Not my will, but yours. Not my words, but yours. Not my worth, but yours. Not my glory, but yours. Not in my name, but in yours."

Somewhere we know that without a lonely place, our lives are in danger. Somewhere we know that without silence, words lose their meaning; that without listening, speaking no longer heals; that without distance, closeness cannot cure. Somewhere we know that without a solitary place, our actions quickly become empty gestures. The careful balance between silence and words, withdrawal and involvement, distance and closeness, solitude and community forms the basis of the spiritual life and should therefore be the subject of our most personal attention.

PRAYER IS DESCENDING FROM MIND TO HEART

Theophan the Recluse, the nineteenth-century Russian mystic mentioned in the introduction, summarized the Hesychast tradition of interior prayer[2] when he said: "To pray is to descend with the mind into the heart, and there to stand before the face of the Lord, ever-present, all-seeing, within you."[3] When our mind has become full of the Lord, and when our heart is empty, we can descend with our mind into our heart—that point of our being where there are no divisions or distinctions and where we are totally one. In order to move from mind to heart, or "from unceasing thinking to unceasing prayer," we have to embrace solitude and silence and then find God in the center of our being. There, in the place of the heart, we learn to listen attentively to the One who calls us "my beloved."[4]

If theological reflection is an openness of one's mind to God's truth and wisdom, spiritual formation is the openness of one's heart in gratitude to God and God's people. Both require a radical receptivity to God's great gift of life and a consistent spiritual practice to slowly create space for God to be revealed. It is in this poverty of mind and heart that we can receive in gratitude the life of the Spirit within.

How do we concretely move from head to heart? When I lie in my bed, not able to fall asleep because of my many words and worries; when I am preoccupied with all the things that I must do or that can go wrong; when I can't take my mind off my concern for a needy or dying friend—what am I supposed to do? Pray? Fine, but how do I do this?

One simple way is by slowly repeating a particular prayer with as much attentiveness as possible. Focused prayer, first in the mind and then repeated in the heart, becomes easier the more you practice. When you know the "Our Father," the "Glory Be to God," or the "Lord Have Mercy" by heart, you have something to start with. Just begin praying those prayers repeatedly. You might like to learn by heart the Twenty-third Psalm ("The Lord is my shepherd. . . ."), or Paul's words about love to the Corinthians, or the Prayer of St. Francis ("Lord, make me an instrument of your peace . . ."). As you lie in bed, drive your car, wait for the bus, or walk your dog, you can slowly let the words of one of these prayers go through your mind down to your heart by trying to listen with your whole being to what you are repeating. You may be distracted by your worries, but if you keep going back to the words of the prayer, you will gradually discover that your worries become less obsessive, your attention becomes more focused, and you really start to enjoy praying. As the prayer descends from your mind into the center of your being, you will discover its healing power.

PRAYER IS THE PRACTICE OF THE PRESENT MOMENT

Prayer, the discipline of the heart, is a spiritual practice of the present moment. Jean-Pierre de Caussade, in his three-hundred-year-old spiritual classic, *The Sacrament of the Present Moment,* assures us that God speaks to us through every moment of every day:

> If we understood how to see in each moment some manifestation of the will of God we should find therein also all that our hearts could desire. . . . The present is ever filled with infinite treasure, it contains more than you have capacity to hold. Faith is the measure. Believe, and it will be done to you accordingly.

When we abandon ourselves to God in prayer, then each moment becomes a sacrament of joy, gratitude, and loving acceptance of the will of God manifest in that moment. By embracing the present moment of contemplation, and facing ourselves honestly and openly in prayer, God will grant us our heart's desire: The more the heart loves, the more it desires; and the more it desires, so much the more will it receive. The will of God is at each moment before us like an immense, inexhaustible ocean that no human heart can fathom; but none can receive from it more than he has capacity to contain, it is necessary to enlarge this capacity by faith, confidence, and love.[5]

Practicing the presence of God in the present moment also is the gift Brother Lawrence gave us through his example of constant prayer in the midst of ordinary, daily activities. As a cook for his monastic community in Paris in the late seventeenth century, Brother Lawrence simply and beautifully explains how to "pray without ceasing"—not from the head but from the heart. In his little book *The Practice of the Presence of God,* Lawrence said that it was a great delusion to separate times of prayer from other times. Rather, we are to pray by being aware of the presence of God at all times and places. Brother Lawrence found no difference between the appointed times of prayer and times for work.[6] Thus, anyone who seeks to know God's peace and presence, regardless of age or circumstance, can practice—anywhere, anytime—the sacrament of the present moment.[7]

When we pray, we enter into the presence of God whose name is Immanuel—God-with-us. To pray is to listen attentively to the One who addresses us here and now. When we dare to trust that we are never alone but that God is always with us, always cares for us, and always speaks to us, we can gradually detach ourselves from the voices that make us feel guilty or anxious, and embrace the present moment. If we could, for a few minutes each day, just be fully where we are, we would indeed discover that we are not alone, and that the One who is with us in our hearts wants only to give us the love we need and the power to love others.

WHAT HAPPENS WHEN WE TAKE TIME TO PRAY?

Just as we have our set times to eat, work, play, and rest, so also do we need regular times to pray. Why not get up early enough to spend at least half an hour with God, and then some gentle time with those with whom we live. The best time to pray is the early morning, because praying then helps us to live the rest of the day more God centered. But if that is unrealistic, set aside some other time during the day when God gets our full attention. Any half hour during the day is better than no time at all.

Once we have set aside a time to pray, we also need to set aside a place for prayer. A quiet, peaceful place is essential for good prayer. Jesus invited us: "Go to your private room, shut yourself in, and so pray to your Father who is in that secret place" (Matt. 6:6). Jesus makes it clear that not only time but also space belongs to the discipline of prayer. The ideal place is a special room in your house set aside for prayer. When such a room is decorated with images that speak about God, when there are some candles to light, even some incense to burn, you more easily will want to pray there. And the more you pray in such a place, the more the place will be filled with the energy of prayer.

If you don't have a spare room for prayer, at least reserve a little corner of your room for prayer. If that is not possible, try to go to a church or chapel where you feel safe and where you desire to return. A place that you visit daily for prayer soon becomes a friendly place, a place that gently calls you back to prayer and welcomes you with open arms whenever you walk in.

What do you do once you have set aside a time and a place to be alone with God? The simple answer is: just be with Jesus. Let him look at you, touch you, and speak to you; and look, touch, and speak to him in your own way, in any way your heart desires.

Without the discipline of prayer, the world retains its illusions. Without an hour of public prayers, or a half hour of private prayer, or ten minutes of quiet meditation, or saying a brief prayer of gratitude before or after a meal, we forget that God is present in the world and in our life. When we remember to pray in the morning, when we are mindful of the present moment, when we set apart Saturday or Sunday as the Sabbath, God's special day of the week, then all of life, and all times and places, and all people that we see are transformed by the light of God. The more we pray—in the sense of living a prayerful life—the more we desire to be with God in prayer. Prayer creates in us a hunger and thirst to be with the One whom we have seen shining through nature and moments in time, people, and events.

When we turn our hearts to God in prayer, we will not only see ourselves as loved by God, but see other people in the light of God's great love. The heart of God is not only the place where we find our true selves, but also the place where we find men, women, and children of all times and places and discover that they, too, are our brothers and sisters, loved as uniquely and completely as we are loved. In the heart of God we find the true joy of being part of the human race. There we are truly connected, not only with God, but with ourselves and with one another. Thus prayer becomes "the only necessary thing" (Luke 10:42).

DEALING WITH DISTRACTIONS

One of the interesting things that happen when we spend time with God in prayer is that we find out how tired and anxious we are. If we don't fall asleep, we find out how full our head is of worries and concerns and things we need to do. While we are trying to be with God, we are busy thinking about all the plans we have made. A thousand distractions will come our way, like jumping monkeys filling a banana tree. As soon as we enter into solitude, we discover how chaotic our inner life is. Suddenly all sorts of thoughts, feelings, and fantasies come to the surface, and we soon find ourselves thinking about old pains and old rewards, about appointments we forgot to keep and letters we forgot to write, about people we hope to see and people we hope we never see, about a future vacation, a possible promotion, or our approaching retirement. Instead of being prayerful we become restless and can't wait until our half hour is over.

Don't be surprised at this. You can't just suddenly shut the door of a house that was always open to strangers and expect no one to knock on the door. It will take a while for these countless distractions to disappear, but eventually they will, especially when they realize that you refuse to open the door to them for at least half an hour. If we faithfully keep our time of prayer, every single day, then slowly the distractions diminish and our mind and body join in a rhythm of daily prayer.

We all need help to stay focused. We cannot just sit there in silence and do nothing—at least not at first. We need a focus, a point of concentration. This is true in all faith traditions and spiritual practices: by focusing on one thing, we fight distractions. We do not fight distractions by pushing things away; rather, we fight them by focusing on one thing. It's like looking at a candle for a long time. Slowly we start feeling quiet as we focus on something, and all other things begin to disappear.

To help you focus, pick a sacred text: the gospel lesson of the day, the Our Father, the Beatitudes, the Prayer of St. Francis, or any words that come from God and speak to your heart. Gently focus your thoughts on these sacred words you have chosen. When the distractions come, smile at them, let them pass, and return to your chosen text. The words spoken with your lips or silently in your heart will become increasingly attractive to you, and soon you will find them much more important than the many "oughts," "musts," and "have to's" that try to slip into your consciousness and create havoc there. Words that come from God have the power to transform your inner life and create there a home where God gladly dwells.

In all of this don't forget about your body. Give it a quiet time to rest and a peaceful place to pray. Let it sit, stand, kneel, or lie prostrate in the presence of God. Even if your heart is not ready to be fully there, when your body is engaged in an attitude of worship and adoration, your heart eventually will discover that it doesn't have to wander off but can come home where the body is and enter gladly with it into the presence of God. Once your mind, heart, and body are reunited in prayer, your whole life will become one act of thanksgiving and praise. Then, when your time for prayer is done and you must leave your special place, you will remain prayerful at all times and places, and will be filled with the presence of God. I am not presenting you with an easy goal, but a goal that corresponds to your deepest desire and is within your reach.

CONCLUSION

The movement from illusion to prayer requires a persistent discipline and daily practice.

When our minds reach out to eternity, when our hearts reach out to the love of God and our bodies set the boundaries that prevent us from falling constantly back on the narrowing compulsions, obsessions, and addictions of our world, we will stop being like chickens picking out the dirty leftovers of their past needs and be, instead, like eagles soaring high on the wings of God, grateful for our freedom and able to enjoy the unspeakable beauty of our spiritual existence.

GOING DEEPER:
EXERCISES FOR
SPIRITUAL FORMATION

Nouwen repeatedly called for setting apart a sacred time and place each day to "make space for God" in our innermost being. In the disciplines of solitude and silence, Nouwen taught, the heart finds communion with God in prayer. And, as he wrote in *The Way of the Heart,* the "purification and transformation that take place in solitary prayer manifest themselves in compassion."[8]

REFLECT AND JOURNAL

1. Mother Teresa is best known for her example of compassion for the "poorest of the poor." Those who know her best know that her compassion was the fruit of hours of "useless" prayer. Ponder the following familiar quote by Mother Teresa in light of the invitation to pray: "I'm not called to be successful; I'm called to be faithful."

2. Reflect on the following paragraph from Caussade's *Sacrament of the Present Moment:*

> There is not a moment in which God does not present Godself under the cover of some pain to be endured, of some consolation to be enjoyed, or of some duty to be performed. All that takes place

within us, around us, or through us, contains and conceals God's divine action. It is really and truly there present, but invisibly present, so that we are always surprised and do not recognize God's operation until it has ceased. If we could lift the veil, and if we were attentive and watchful God would continually reveal Godself to us, and we should see God's divine action in everything that happened to us, and rejoice in it. At each successive occurrence we should exclaim: "It is the Lord," and we should accept every fresh circumstance as a gift of God.[9]

GUIDELINES FOR SOLITARY PRAYER

Here are Nouwen's guidelines for solitary prayer—three simple ways to move from life's illusions to the heart of prayer in everyday life.[10]

First, Be Silent
Solitude and silence are the heart of contemplative prayer. But I find it hard to be silent alone, because the distractions are so many. To be silent together with another is very helpful. Read together with a friend, and then be silent together.

Focus on the Word of God
In the daily discipline of prayer our focus is on God and the words of God. You can read a Psalm or a very short section of scripture. Simply take a passage and read it two or three times, and keep your mind focused on that passage. Do not think about it in terms of analyzing it, but simply become aware of what that passage presents to you. The text may show you Jesus healing someone or speaking with the disciples. That image of Jesus

before you becomes your focus. This is called *lectio divina*, and it is a very simple and powerful way to pray. Or, focus on a certain word or phrase that stands out in the passage. When you are distracted, just return to the image or the word that you focused on. After reading a passage of scripture, take a bite, so to speak, out of the text. For instance, take a very short sentence like "The Lord is my shepherd." For ten minutes of meditation, do nothing at all but say, "The Lord is my shepherd, the Lord is my shepherd, the Lord is my shepherd." Slowly this truth becomes flesh in us. Repeating the phrase several times quiets us down and allows our mind to descend into our heart. The words quietly spoken become a hedge around a garden in which God's shepherding can be sensed. There we are with the Lord who becomes our loving shepherd who leads us to silent pastures where it is safe to dwell. This method is called *meditative prayer*.

Pray Without Ceasing

You may have heard about the famous "Jesus Prayer"—"Lord Jesus Christ, Son of David, have mercy on me a sinner"—from the Gospel of Luke (18:38). Those ancient biblical words were shortened and repeated very slowly in the Hesychast tradition of interior prayer. When these words are repeated daily, they become a part of our breathing, part of our heartbeat, part of our whole way of being. The beautiful thing about the Jesus Prayer is that we can take this practice with us into our daily activities and pray it while we drive a car, sit behind a desk, or work on our feet. "Lord Jesus Christ, have mercy on me . . ." or "Lord, have mercy . . ." or "O God, mercy . . ." repeated throughout the day is one way of fulfilling the scriptural command to "pray without ceasing" (1 Thess. 5:17). This is called the *prayer of the heart*.

GUIDELINES FOR MORNING
AND EVENING PRAYERS

Here are Nouwen's guidelines for group prayer in the mornings and evenings.[11]

> I think a person's prayer life should be a little public. That sounds like the opposite of what the gospel says, but it is not meant to be. I mean "public" in the sense that it's okay for people to know that there are certain times of the day or night that you have set apart for prayer, either alone or with others who enjoy being silent together in prayer.

> For morning prayers, I have a simple formula that anyone can follow. I read three Psalms out loud, and then a reading from the New Testament, followed by ten minutes of silent meditation. Then I pray another Psalm and read a contemporary text of some sort, followed by another ten minutes of silence. Then I pray a concluding prayer and the Our Father. It takes less than one hour, and the nice thing about such a format is that I can always invite a friend: "This is what I do in the mornings, would you like to join me?"

> For evening prayers, I like to sit in a circle with friends and chant the Psalms. If you are having a dinner party, you simply tell your guests: "At 10 P.M., I have my evening prayers. If you would like to join me, please do. Otherwise, I would like to finish dinner in time." People will not say, "Oh, gosh, why this?" Rather, people will tend to respond favorably and enjoy seeing you stick to your commitments.

Visio Divina: The Useless Tree

If you are learning to pray, imagine yourself sitting on the bench at Saint-Rémy de Provence, under a tall old tree as painted by the famous Dutch artist Vincent van Gogh.[12] (See color insert.) Reread the parable that opens this chapter, and ask yourself these questions: How is this tree useful? How is it useless? How does it glorify God in its branches and shade? Can all creation praise God by simply being what it was created to be? Consider these questions, and then simply look at the image for ten minutes, letting the image speak to you. Write down your thoughts and reflections.

Like the old tree in the parable, we don't pray to be productive or useful, but to become open and grateful. In prayer and meditation, we can live and be; we can bear or not bear fruit, and we can grow old freely, without being preoccupied with our usefulness. Faithfulness in prayer is its own reward, with or without tangible results.

PART TWO

Midlife Movements

THREE

From Sorrow to Joy

~ The Tale of Kisa Gotami and
the Mustard Seeds ~

Kisa Gotami, called the Frail One, had a young son who was the sunshine of her day. It came to pass that hardly had he grown big enough to run and play, when he died. So great was the sorrow of Kisa Gotami that she would not accept the boy's death. Instead she took to the streets, carrying her dead son on her hip. She went forth from house to house, knocking at each door and demanding: "Give me medicine for my son." People saw that she was mad. They made fun of her and told her: "There is no medicine for the dead." But she acted as if she did not understand, and only went on asking.

Now a certain wise old man saw Kisa Gotami and understood that it was her sorrow for the dead son that had driven her out of her mind. He did not mock her, but instead told her: "Woman, the only one who might know of medicine for your son is the Possessor of the Ten Forces, he who is foremost among men and gods. Go then to the monastery. Go then to him, and ask him about medicine for your son."

Seeing that the wise man spoke the truth, she went with her son on her hip to the monastery in which the Buddha resided. Eagerly, she approached the seat of the Buddhas where the Teacher sat. "I wish to have medicine for my son, Exalted One," she said.

Smiling serenely, the Buddha answered: "It is well that you have come here. This is what you must do. You must go to each house in the city, one by one, and from each you must seek to fetch tiny grains of mustard seed. But not just any house will do. You must only take mustard seeds from those houses in which no one has ever died."

Gotami agreed at once and delightedly set out to re-enter the city. At the first house she knocked and asked, saying: "It is I, Gotami, sent by the Possessor of the Ten Forces. You are to give me tiny grains of mustard seed. This is the medicine I must have for my son." And when they brought her the mustard seed, she added: "Before I take the seed, tell me, is this a house in which no one has died?" "Oh no, Gotami," they answered, "the dead from this house are beyond counting." "Then I must go elsewhere," said Gotami, "the Exalted One was very clear about this. I am to seek out mustard seeds only from those houses which death has not visited."

On she went from one house to the next. But always the same answer. In the entire city there was no house which death had not touched. Finally she understood why she had been sent on this hopeless mission. She left the city, overcome with her feeling, and carried her dead son to the burning-ground. There she gave him up.

Returning to the monastery, she was greeted by the

softly smiling Buddha, who asked her: "Good Gotami, did you fetch the tiny grains of mustard seed from the house without death, as I told you to?"

And Gotami answered: "Most honored sir, there are no houses where death is not known. All mankind is touched by death. My own dear son is dead. But I see now that whoever is born must die. Everything passes away. There is no medicine for this but acceptance of it. There is no cure but the knowing. My search is over for the mustard seeds. You, O Possessor of the Ten Forces, have given me refuge. Thank you, my Exalted One."

—"A Tale from *The Teachings of the Compassionate Buddha*"[1]

The ancient Buddhist tale about how the woman Kisa Gotami overcame her deep sorrow and loss embodies for me the movement from denial to acceptance and from sorrow to joy. If there is any word that summarizes the sorrows of life, it is the word *loss*. We are sad because of all we have lost. Some of the losses that settle deeply in our hearts are the loss of intimacy through separations, the loss of safety through violence, the loss of innocence through abuse, the loss of friends through betrayal, the loss of love through abandonment, the loss of home through war, the loss of well-being through hunger, heat, and cold, the loss of children through illness or accidents, the loss of country through political upheaval, and the loss of life through earthquakes, floods, plane crashes, bombings, and diseases.

Think about your own losses right now—the many places in your life where you have lost something dear and life giving. You may have lost a friend to cancer, a child to disease, a spouse to death. Maybe a longtime relationship came to a painful end. Someone you loved deeply died suddenly. You may have lost your house or your job in troubled times. Because of emotional or physical abuse, you may feel broken. Whatever your loss, you are not alone in experiencing it.

Life sometimes seems like just one long series of losses. When you are born you lose the safety and intimacy of your mother's womb. When you go to school you lose the intimacy and security of your family life. When you get your first job you lose the freedom of youth. If you marry, you lose the joy of many options. When you grow old you lose your good looks, your health, your friends, your money, or your fame. And when you die, you physically lose it all!

In the afternoon and evening of life, there are also painful losses through conflict, misunderstanding, failure, anger, and resentment. There is the loss of our hopes and dreams, not only through age, but also through the discovery of corruption and betrayal among people we have trusted for a long time. There is the loss of meaning and purpose in our lives, not only because our minds and hearts become tired, but also because long-cherished ways of thinking and praying are suddenly ridiculed or considered old-fashioned. You can say that each of us somehow loses "the good old days," which might not have been as good as we think, but which somehow are locked into our memories as foundation stones of our lives.

When we were young, we said, "This is what I'm going to do with my life." When we grew old, we said, "What happened to the dream?" When we were young, we wanted to do something great for humanity. Now we may feel stuck in a job, bored with our work, or lost in retirement. Our enthusiasm has waned. We feel that life has disappointed us or that there is not much new to discover.

These many losses are part of ordinary life. But beyond the ordinary there may be a spiritual loss—a loss of hope for the future, the loss of divine purpose in life, even the loss of faith in God. When you were younger, you could bear your losses with fortitude, trusting that they would bring you closer to God. The pain and suffering of life were bearable because you lived them as ways to test your willpower and deepen your conviction. But as you grew older, you discovered that what supported you for so many years—your faith in God, your love for Jesus, your trust in family and friends, your hope in life—was diminished. Long-cherished ideas, long-practiced disciplines, and long-held customs of celebrating life now no longer warm your heart.

You may remember a time long ago when Jesus was so real for you and you had no doubt about his presence in your life. Once he was your dearest and most intimate friend, counselor, and guide. He gave you comfort, courage, and confidence. You could feel him—yes, taste and touch him. And now? What happened? You no longer feel him in your life or think of him very much. You no longer desire to spend an hour in his presence. You even wonder if he was ever more than just a figure out of a storybook or in your imagination. I am not suggesting that all of these losses will touch each of our lives in the same way. But as we walk together and listen to each other, we will soon discover that many, if not most, of these losses are part of the human journey—our own journey or the journey of our companions.

What to do with our losses? That's the big question that faces us. Is there a way for that which is lost to be found? Can sadness turn to gladness? Can mourning lead to dancing? When "weeping lasts for a night time," does joy truly come in the morning (Ps. 30:5)?

MOURN YOUR LOSSES

The question is not whether you have experienced loss, but rather how you live your losses. Are you hiding them? Are you pretending they aren't real? Are you refusing to share them with your fellow travelers? Are you trying to convince yourself that your losses are little compared with your gains? Are you blaming someone for what you have suffered and lost?

There is another option—the possibility of mourning. Yes,

you can mourn your losses. You cannot talk or act them away, but you can shed tears over them and allow yourself to grieve deeply. You can never get to the joy if you dare not cry, if you do not have the courage to weep, if you don't take the opportunity to experience the pain. The world says, "Just ignore it, be strong, don't cry, get over it, move on." But if you don't mourn you can become bitter. All your grief can go right into your deepest self and sit there for the rest of your life.

Better to mourn your losses than to deny them. Dare to feel your losses. Dare to grieve them. Name the pain and say, "Yes, I feel real pain, real fear, real loss; and I am going to embrace it. I will take up the cross of my life, and accept it." To grieve is to experience the pain of your life and face the dark abyss where nothing is clear or settled, where everything is shifting and changing. To fully grieve is to allow your losses to tear apart feelings of false security and safety and lead you to the painful truth of your brokenness and dependence upon God alone. Finally, you come to the point where you honestly can say: "Yes, yes, yes! This is my life, and I accept it."

I have mourned many losses in my life. How well I remember the day my mother died, and how I felt after her illness and death. It changed my experience of time. Every "normal" occasion of life became a new experience, like a "first time." The first Christmas without mother, the first New Year's without her, the first Easter. I could hardly remember any family events without her being part of them. I could no longer predict how I would feel on one of these familiar days and occasions. Every time I lived through another event without her, I felt her absence in a new way. And each time, she died again in me. Yet, right when I was weeping, right when I was experiencing my deepest sadness—right in the middle of all that, something new was happening. Right there in the pain, I began to get in touch with a joy that was deeper and more profound. In human brokenness new life is born. In the tears and grief, joy and happiness are found.

True healing begins at the moment that we can face the reality of our losses and let go of the illusions of control.[2]

Since we are such fearful people, the hardest challenge we face is the reality of our losses and how to let go of the illusion of control, the challenge to go beyond our fears and to trust that one day we will be liberated from the bonds that hold us captive. I don't think we can do this by relying solely on our intellectual and emotional abilities. If our own human capacities are our sole resources, it would seem that the only reasonable response to our losses would be some form of stoicism. But I do believe that the Spirit of Jesus, the Spirit of Love, is given to us to reach out beyond our fears and embrace the reality of our losses. This is what mourning is all about: allowing the pain of our losses to enter our hearts; having the courage to let our wounds be known to ourselves and felt by ourselves; embracing the freedom to cry in anguish, or to scream in protest—and so to risk being led into an inner space where the joy can be found.

There's a "time to weep, and a time to laugh; a time to mourn and a time to dance" (Eccles. 3:4). But what I want to tell you is that these *times* are connected. Mourning and dancing are part of the same movement of grace. Somehow, in the midst of your tears, a gift of life is given. Somehow, in the midst of your mourning, the first steps of the dance take place. The cries that well up from your losses belong to your song of praise. Those who cannot grieve cannot be joyful. Those have not been sad cannot be glad. Quite often, right in the midst of your crying, your smile comes through your tears. And while you are mourning, you already are working on the choreography of your dance. Your tears of grief have softened your spirit and opened up the possibility to say "thanks." You can claim your unique journey as God's way to mold your heart and bring you joy.

CONNECT YOUR PAIN TO THE LARGER STORY

If the first step on the journey from sorrow to joy is to face and mourn your losses, the second step is this: Connect your suffering with that of the larger world. See your losses in light of the suffering of others.

When I came to Daybreak, I was in a great deal of personal pain.[3] My many years in the academic world, my travels among the poor in Central America, and my busy speaking schedule left me spiritually depleted. Rather than providing an escape from my own inner conflicts, my scurrying from one continent to another had only intensified my inner turmoil. I clung to the illusion that I was in control, that I could avoid what I did not want to face within myself and in the world around me. As I witnessed the enormous suffering of people with mental and physical handicaps at Daybreak, I gradually came to see my own painful problems in a new light. I realized they formed part of a much larger story of suffering. I found through that insight new energy to live amid my own hardship and pain. I realized that healing begins with taking your pain out of its diabolic isolation and seeing that whatever we suffer, we suffer in communion with all of humanity, and, yes, all of creation. In so doing, we become participants in the great battle against the powers of darkness. Our little lives participate in something much larger and universal.

I found something else: among these people, most of whom cannot read, many of whom cannot care for themselves, among men and women rejected by a world that values only the whole and bright and healthy, I saw people learning how to make the connection between human suffering and God's suffering. When I saw the connection, I longed to be part of it. I wanted to connect my pain with the pain of all these people. Suddenly, I knew, "I am part of humanity!" I am not the great exception. I suffer as other people suffer. I cry like other people cry, and I can dance as other people dance. Suddenly I realized that, yes, I want to live this truth together, I want to live it in community.

Community and solidarity are at the heart of the movement from sorrow to joy. When you begin to feel the pain of your life in relation to other people's pain, you can face it together. This is where the word *compassion* comes from (*com-passion* = passion, to suffer, to suffer with, to suffer with other persons); that's where the word *patience* comes from (*patience* = *patior*, "to suffer"). To be patient is to experience the pain of your life. And when you experience it with somebody else, you can be compassionate. This is how the healing begins. Not by wonderful answers, not by "do this or do that." It starts by experiencing the powerlessness of *not-knowing-what-to-do* together. That is why it's so important that we grow in compassion. As we feel and live the pain of our own losses, our grieving hearts open to a wider world of suffering and loss—to a world of prisoners, refugees, AIDS patients, starving children, and the countless human beings living in constant fear. Then the pain of our life connects us with the moaning and groaning of a suffering humanity.

The spiritual question is whether you can live your pain in solidarity with other people who also suffer. Can you say, "Yes, this is part of being human, and I share it with thousands and millions of people and with people who are born before me, with people who lived long before me, and with people who will live long after me"? Can you say, "Somehow I am a part of the great story of God's salvation. And I want to connect with the long struggle of humanity. I want to live my suffering—not isolated, but connected with the great human drama of love where sorrow and joy are experienced together"?

I invite you to live consciously connected to this great struggle of existence and faith in God's love and deliverance. If you have a friend who is in pain or who has lost someone, can you just listen and say, "I love you and will be with you, I want to hear how hard it is. I don't know what to say to you, I don't know what to do about it, but I do want to be with you, and walk with you. I am not afraid. I am not going to say something cheery about the bad and that there is something better beyond. I just want to be here with you now and say: Yes! You have lost something, someone, and it hurts like hell, and you are not alone"?

If your family or community is suffering, I want you to feel the pain together and find the joy hidden in the midst of the pain. I invite you to be together in the struggle. The way we let go of our losses and sorrows is by connecting our personal pain to the great suffering of humanity, by understanding our own grief and loss as part of the larger picture of the world. For we are not the only ones who suffer in the world. Nor are we alone.

DISCOVER THE ONE WHO WALKS BESIDE YOU

"The Road to Emmaus" is a familiar Easter story about Jesus and his disciples in the Gospel of Luke,[4] but on a deeper level, it is about the movement from sorrow to joy. Like the journey of Kisa Gotami, the journey of the disciples to Emmaus helps us to travel interiorly, from the place of sadness and loss to the place of joy and thanksgiving. I want you to try to hear and feel this story at its deepest level.[5]

Two people are walking together. You can see from the way they walk that they are not happy. Their bodies are bent over, their faces are downcast, their movements are slow. They do not look at each other. Previously, they felt sad, empty, depressed, perhaps disillusioned, grieving that their Master was gone and that their life together had not turned out as planned.

It was only a few years ago that they met someone who had changed their lives, someone who had radically interrupted their daily routines and brought a new vitality to every part of their existence. They had left their village, followed that stranger and his friends, and discovered a whole new reality hidden behind the veil of their ordinary activities—a reality in which forgiveness, healing, and love were no longer mere words but powers touching the very core of their humanity. The stranger from Nazareth had made everything new. He had made them into people for whom the world was no longer a burden but a challenge, no longer a field of snares but a place with endless opportunities. He had brought joy and peace to their daily experience. He had made their life into a dance! Now he is dead and gone. His body, which had radiated light, has been destroyed under the hands of his torturers. They have lost him. Not just him, but with him, also themselves. The energy that had filled their days and nights has left them, and they feel completely empty. They have become two lost human beings, walking home without having a home, returning to what has become a dark memory.

As the two travelers walk home mourning their loss, Jesus comes up and walks by their side. But the pain they feel prevents them from recognizing him. "We've lost it all, we lost our hopes, we lost our joy, we lost our Master. Don't you know what happened? The one we really thought was going to give us life is dead, he's gone, it's over!"

Jesus does not say, "Oh, don't worry. It will all be okay. No, he says, "Tell me, tell me about your pain, show me your grief, I want to feel your anguish. I want to be with you, I want to listen to your story."

What happens next? Jesus says something very remarkable. He says, "You foolish people." I don't think he meant "you stupid people." No, it is a much more tender remark than that. "Foolish people," he says softly. "So slow to believe." These words go straight to the hearts of the two disciples. *Foolish* is a hard word, a word that offends us and makes us defensive. But it can also crack open a cover of fear and self-consciousness and lead to a whole new knowledge of being human. It is a wake-up call, a ripping off of blindfolds, a tearing down of useless protective devices. You foolish people, don't you see—don't you hear—don't you know? You have been looking at a little bush and not realizing that you are on the top of a mountain that offers you a worldwide view. You have been complaining about your losses, not realizing that these losses are there to enable you to receive the gift of life. The stranger has to call them "foolish" in order to make them see. Suddenly something happens! The story shifts. The stranger begins to speak, and his words command serious attention. He has listened to *them;* now they are able to listen to *him.*

Jesus talked about Abraham, Moses, and the Prophets, and he talked about the great story of human suffering that led to something new: "Don't you know that Abraham had to leave his land and go to a new place? Don't you know that Moses had to get out of Egypt and live in the desert with his people? Don't you know that the Prophets all talk about who is suffering, and invite us all to live in new ways together? Don't you know about all the times that I had to suffer, and that you will suffer, and that we will have to struggle together? Don't you realize that it's the way of salvation, of hope, of re-creation? Don't you get that the grain has to die? Because if it does not die it will simply remain a grain. But if it dies it will bear fruit. Don't you know that you have to lose your life, and thus gain it?" All this is said not as a criticism or to create fear, but simply as *revelation.*

Jesus joins us as we walk in sadness and grief, and opens the scriptures to us. On our journey, he explains how the passages are about him. Whether we read the book of Exodus, the Psalms, the Prophets, or the Gospels, they are all there to touch our hearts. But we don't know that it is Jesus with us on the road. We think of him as a stranger who knows less than we do of what is happening in our lives. And still—we know something, we sense something: our hearts begin to burn within us. At the very moment that he is with us we can't fully understand what is happening. Later, sometimes much later, when it is all over, we might be able to say, "Did not our hearts burn within us as he talked to us on the road and explained the scriptures to us?" But at the time when he walks and talks with us, it is all too close and too soon for reflection.

The loss, the grief, the guilt, the fear, the glimpses of hope, and the many unanswered questions that battled for attention in their restless minds—all of these were lifted up by this stranger and placed in the context of a story much larger than their own. What had seemed so confusing began to offer new horizons; what had seemed so oppressive began to feel like a coming liberation; what had seemed so extremely sad began to take on the quality of joy! As he talked to them, they gradually came to know that their little lives weren't as little as they had thought, but part of a great mystery that not only embraced many generations, but stretched itself out from eternity to eternity.

The stranger didn't say that there was no reason for sadness, but that their sadness was part of a larger sadness in which joy was hidden. The stranger didn't say that the death they were mourning wasn't real, but that it was a death that inaugurated new life—real life. The stranger didn't say that they hadn't lost a friend who had given them courage and hope, but that this loss would create the way to a new relationship far beyond any friendship they had ever experienced. Never did the stranger deny what they told him. Rather, he affirmed it as part of a much larger event in which they were allowed to play a unique role.

As they listened to the stranger, something changed within the two sad travelers. Not only did they sense a new hope and a new joy touching their innermost being, but their walk became more determined and purposeful. The stranger had given them a new sense of direction. And their hearts started to burn.

If you want to discover this truth in your heart, you have to see your life as a little part of a greater story. You have to see that your life now is part of what others throughout history have lived before you, and will live after you. That what you are experiencing now, in the loss of your friends, your family, your expectations of Jesus, is something that is part of an enormously large story of losses past, present, and future. And that new life and greater joy will come.

I hope that is happening in you right now. As you begin to let go of your own private pain and loss, as you begin to connect your story to the greater mystery, and as you start to feel Christ's presence in the Word that opens to you, does not your heart burn within you? Do you not feel inner warmth beginning to glow? Do you not hear, faintly at first, the inner Voice of Love? Once you hear and start to trust the One who speaks your name, you will know that it is the Lord who speaks to you. Jesus is his name.[6]

CONCLUSION

The first step in the movement from sorrow to joy is to face and mourn your losses. The second step is to connect your suffering with that of the larger world, to see your losses in light of the suffering of others. In time you may be able to be thankful that you are not alone but a part of a larger humanity that struggles with you, that groans for a new world to be revealed. On the road to Emmaus, Jesus becomes present through the scriptures. It is that patient, unmaking presence that transforms sadness to joy and turns mourning to dancing.

GOING DEEPER: EXERCISES FOR SPIRITUAL FORMATION

Read the story of Jesus on the road to Emmaus in Luke 24:13–35.

Practice *lectio divina* of the passage by reading it aloud, slowly and in the company of others, three times, noting for further reflection which word, phrase, or image calls for your attention.

REFLECT AND JOURNAL

1. Can you identify with one of the disciples who are grieving the loss of their Master as they walk home to Emmaus? Can you imagine a stranger on the road who listens and understands your pain? Can you invite him into your home to sit down at table? Can you see how he breaks bread in a particular way? Is he the One who can turn your sadness to joy and warm your heart again?

2. How have you discovered the One who walks beside you? From your journal, share with another a time when you recognized the presence of Jesus in the scriptures, or in the breaking of bread, or in the gift of companionship.

3. According to Nouwen, the story of the disciples on the road to Emmaus has five parts; that is, the movement from mourning to dancing involves five steps:

    1. Mourning your losses

    2. Connecting your own sufferings with the great sufferings of humanity

    3. Inviting the "one" whom you recognize on the road into your house

    4. Entering into communion with the Christ living in you

    5. Going into the world with joy

    Which step are you practicing at the present moment? Which one would you like to try?

4. What have you learned from the story of the enlightenment of Kisa Gotami? Note that the sorrow of Kisa Gotami was so overwhelming and devastating that she went mad. Walking aimlessly on the streets, carrying her dead son on her hip, she went from house to house, demanding, "Give me medicine for my son." People mocked her for refusing to accept the reality of her son's death. Her cure was in discovering that death and loss are universal, that "there are no houses where death is not known." The medicine for her grief was found in her identification with others who also suffered. Her search for the cure in the mustard seeds was found in recognizing the "Exalted One," in whom she found refuge. Once enlightened, Gotami was able to practice what Buddhists sometimes call *infinite resignation:* "I see now that whoever is born must die. Everything passes away. There is no medicine for this but acceptance of it. There is no cure but the knowing." Many

travelers have learned that the movement away from grief and sorrow begins with mourning our losses. That sorrow builds kinship with all people. That just as the "frail one" in the story, in a time of overwhelming sorrow, came to accept her son's death, so we are called to embrace our sorrows and finally let go of our pain and loss. For Christians, this spiritual recognition is found in the risen Christ who meets us, sometimes as a stranger, on our road of life. Our heart is warmed when we are able to discern a "presence" greater than ourselves at work in our life. The Exalted One, the risen Christ, is the One who walks beside us and opens the scriptures to us to reveal the hidden story of our lives. How would you begin to tell your story of loss and what you learned from the experience? How have your own pain and sorrow increased your capacity to help another? How would you reach out with patience and compassion to someone who suffered a devastating loss? Gotami's cure was found in recognizing the "Exalted One." How have you recognized the Exalted One in your life?

A TIME TO MOURN AND A TIME TO DANCE: A MEDITATION ON THE MOVEMENT FROM SORROW TO JOY

In "A Time to Mourn, A Time to Dance" Henri Nouwen offered a meditation for those moving away from sorrow and toward joy.[7] For spiritual practice, try reading the entire meditation out loud, slowly and carefully, emphasizing particular words that catch your attention. You can do this alone or in a group, following the rules for *lectio divina* or for reading poetry.

A Time to Mourn and a Time to Dance

Jesus came to sing a dirge and say: "Cry with me." Jesus came to play a pipe and say: "Dance with me." There is a secret place in us where the Spirit brings new life. There is a crèche where the Child is born in you. There is the broken soil of your soul where the seeds of grace can grow in you. The Spirit of God within us says: "There is a time to mourn and a time to dance." The Spirit of healing that makes us mourn is the same Spirit that makes us dance. The mystery of the dance is that its movements are discovered in the mourning.

A Time to Mourn

Mourn, my people, mourn. Let your pain rise up in your heart and burst forth in you with sobs and cries. Mourn for the silence that exists between you and your spouse. Mourn for the way you were robbed of innocence. Mourn for the absence of a soft embrace, an intimate friendship, a life-giving sexuality. Mourn for the bitterness of your children, the indifference of your friends, and the hardness of heart of your colleagues. Mourn for those whose hunger for love brought them AIDS, whose desire for freedom brought them to refugee camps, whose hunger for justice brought them to prisons. Cry for the millions who die from lack of food, lack of care, lack of love. . . . Cry for freedom, for salvation, for redemption. Cry loudly and deeply, and trust that your tears will make your eyes see that the Kingdom is close at hand—yes, at your fingertips!

A Time to Dance

To heal is to let the Spirit call us to dance. Can you feel the freedom that rises up in you when you have been stripped naked and have nothing to inhibit your movements any-more? You can dance as David danced in front of the Ark. Can you notice in your innermost being the joy of living that comes from having nothing left to lose? Can you see the soft, beautiful smile that appears in the tearful eyes of your mourning friend? Jesus enters into our sadness, takes us by the hand, pulls us gently up to where we can stand, and invites us to dance. And as we dance, we realize that we don't have to stay on the little spot of our grief but can step beyond it into unknown, spacious territory, until we finally know that the entire world is our dance floor. Yes! Leave—leave your father, mother, brother, sister, friend; leave your nets—and you will have many fathers, mothers, brothers, sisters, and friends; all the world will be yours, and you will catch people wherever you dance.

Visio Divina: Sunflowers

As an exercise in sacred seeing, look at the wonderful, exuberant flowers painted by Vincent van Gogh.[8] (See color insert.) What grief, what sadness, what melancholy he experienced in his difficult life. Yet what beauty, what joy, and what ecstasy he was able to embrace. Looking at his vibrant paintings of sunflowers, who can say where the mourning ends and the dance begins? They are never separated. Mourning calls for dancing, dancing for mourning. Glory is hidden in pain. And in this mysterious duality that has become a duet, Vincent celebrates life.

I feel a closeness to Vincent van Gogh, not just because he is also a Dutchman, but because he is a man who really agonized about spiritual questions and therefore has much to say to people who search for God in their lives. Much of his youth was characterized by the struggle to become either a minister or a painter.

But in both vocations, he sought a way to come close to the poor. When he left Borinage, where he lived with the miners, he was on his way to becoming not a preacher worth hearing but a painter worth seeing.

The longer I live, and the more I try to make sense out of my own struggles, the more I find Vincent to be a real companion. One of his favorite expressions was "sorrowful, but always rejoicing." His life and paintings illustrate the three components of the spiritual life. In *solidarity* we cry out with those who suffer. In *consolation* we feel deeply with those in pain. And finally, we offer *comfort* by pointing beyond our shared human pains to glimpses of strength and hope.

When van Gogh left the dark Dutch countryside and, after a short stay in Antwerp, moved to Paris, he became captivated by the bright, gay colors of the city and its surroundings. There he made many studies of flowers and took delight in still-life paintings. Full of enthusiasm, he wrote to his brother, Theo: "It is as if nature starts to burn. In everything there is old gold, bronze, copper . . . a sun, which, for lack of a better word, I must call yellow, sulfur-yellow, soft yellow, lemon-yellow, gold." "Oh!" Vincent wrote to Theo, "those who don't believe in this sun . . . are real infidels. The sun, light in the darkness, light that brightens nature and people, light that calls the dead from their graves. Those who have eyes to see will recognize that all light comes from the same sun." Those who see Vincent's sun will understand his solidarity and consolation and will see the rays of the great sun in their deepest selves.[9]

FOUR

From Resentment to Gratitude

~ The Late Arrivers ~

"Now the kingdom of Heaven is like a landowner going out at daybreak to hire workers for his vineyard. He made an agreement with the workers for one denarius a day and sent them to his vineyard. Going out at about the third hour he saw others standing idle in the market place and said to them, 'You go to my vineyard too and I will give you a fair wage.' So they went. At about the sixth hour and again at about the ninth hour, he went out and did the same. Then at about the eleventh hour he went out and found more men standing around, and he said to them, 'Why have you been standing here idle all day?' 'Because no one has hired us,' they answered. He said to them, 'You go into my vineyard too.' In the evening, the owner of the vineyard said to his bailiff, 'Call the workers and pay them their wages, starting with the last arrivals and ending with the first.' So those who were hired at about the eleventh hour came forward and received one denarius each. When the first came, they expected to get more, but they too received one denarius each. They took it, but grumbled at the landowner saying, 'The men who came last have done only one hour, and you have treated them the same as us, though we have done a heavy day's work in all the heat.' He answered one of them and said, 'My friend, I am not being unjust to you; did we not agree on one denarius? Take your earnings and go. I choose to pay the lastcomer as much as I pay you. Have I no right to do what I like with my own? Why should you be envious because I am generous?' Thus the last will be first, and the first, last."

—Matthew 20:1–16 (New Jerusalem Bible)

I don't know about you, but the parable of the late arrivers angers me greatly![1] Why would the landowner pay those who came for the last hour the same as those who worked the whole day in the vineyard? It's not fair; it's not right. If the landowner did not want to pay the full-day workers *more,* at least he could have paid them *first* and sent them away so that they wouldn't see how much the latecomers got! But no! Right in the face of those early comers who worked the whole day, the landowner pays a day's wage to the latecomers, too, thus creating an occasion for resentment.

Reflecting on this parable, over a long period of time, I have come to realize how self-righteous I am, and how resentful I feel about latecomers receiving the same wage as someone like *me,* an early comer to the vineyard of faith. How easily I forget how great a privilege it is to spend a full day with my brothers and sisters doing what I was asked to do by the One who loves me the most. What prevents me from rejoicing in the landowner's generosity to others? Why am I not grateful for what I received? And for what they received? The movement to be grateful rather than judgmental of others constitutes a profound conversion.[2]

WHAT IS RESENTMENT?

Resentment is a passion, a paralyzing set of complaints that makes us feel angry and frustrated with the people and institutions on which we have made ourselves dependent. *Passion*, in the older sense of the word, is a suffering (pathos = suffering) and a frustration of the power to act rationally due to an overwhelming emotion. Sometimes this helplessness expresses itself in the form of undirected rage or random violence, but more often than not it finds its way onto the compulsive and constraining pathways of resentment. And although resentment is less frightening and less visible than the violent outburst of anger, it is no less destructive.

Each of us knows anger, and how anger is hot. Psychology tells us that if we get in touch with our angry feelings, name them, and sometimes even lash out, the anger loses some of its power over us. We are encouraged to "work with" our anger, enter into our reasons for being upset, and try to engage with those who wound us. This deflating action prevents resentment from building a home in our hearts. But when we swallow our angry feelings and do not make them known, resentment settles in.

Resentment is cold, agonizing anger. When hot anger grows cold it hardens your heart and wreaks havoc in your life. Resentment makes you suspicious, cynical, and depressed. Over the long term, resentment becomes a way of being.

Many of us live with cold anger—the deep feeling that life has let us down, that we suffer unjustly, and that nothing will be done about our complaints. Resentment is one of the most vicious qualities of life because it makes human relationships and community life so difficult. It prevents us from seeking forgiveness and robs us of our joy. It takes away our inner freedom to act creatively and makes us cling to negative feelings as our only way to find an identity. We then become what we are against and regress to the small satisfactions of unexpressed anger. It is from this *passion* that we must be freed in order to live a grateful and *Eucharistic*—that is, a thankful—life.

Resentment often is so deeply hidden that it is not even noticed by those who are most resentful. Resentful people always crave more attention to fuel their negative emotions and, therefore, force others into a defensive stance. In so doing, they close themselves off, making it nearly impossible for others to touch their inner selves. Those of us who give our lives for loved ones, work hard, and have virtues that are praised sometimes are burdened by resentment in our hearts. Resentment is the curse of the faithful, the virtuous, the obedient, and the hardworking.

Ministers who have a great desire to be close to God and serve the people, and those who work in the helping professions, are particularly prone to resentment. They often feel taken advantage of, which can lead to resentment. Religious and social institutions that seek to support ministers and others in the helping professions often serve as breeding grounds for resentment. That is why resentment has been called the most destructive passion in the Christian church.

I remember when I first became aware of the persistence of resentment in the lives of the faithful. In 1973, I was asked to lead a retreat with ten seminarians who were preparing for their ordination to the priesthood. I expected to find a group of vital, highly motivated students full of excitement about their future ministry. I expected a warm welcome and a great eagerness to spend time together discussing the burning issues of Christian ministry. I expected a deep sense of community, developed over the years, expressed authentically in common prayer and Eucharistic celebration. I expected a spirit of gratitude for the many gifts of mind and heart they had received, and an attitude of hopefulness toward new things to come.

None of my expectations were realized. Instead, I encountered a group of tired young students who were wary of yet another talk about religion and just wanted to get through the ordination process. Instead of hospitality, I experienced veiled hostility, subtly expressed by an obvious lack of interest in me in particular and in a church about which they had become cynical. I felt their strong resistance to coming together for a mandatory retreat in a center that long ago must have been full of young people called to the ministry but now seemed to be an empty and sad remembrance of past glory. In their hesitancy to talk about spiritual matters or to pray together, I sensed very little real interest in God or human need. The past was discussed with bitterness and the future with a vague fear of the unknown. When the time came for the final liturgy, there was little to celebrate. Even the guitars could not hide the sham of a Eucharist without genuine thanksgiving.

I do not want to generalize and say that this was the condition of all seminaries or the mood of the whole Church at the time, but I do think it illustrates a perennial paralysis that prevents those with spiritual dreams and great ideals from seeing them realized through institutions. Fertile ground for hope and gratitude can easily become a breeding place for jealousy and resentment. What begins as a life-giving passion of faith and compassion can become a deadly poison without vitality and enthusiasm (from *en theos* = in God).

CAN YOU DRINK THE CUP?

In the Gospel of Matthew we hear the story of the two "sons of Zebedee" who both desired to sit near Jesus when he took his rightful place as long-expected king. So they put their mother up to the task of asking Jesus the question they dared not raise themselves. "Promise me," said the mother of James and John, "that these two sons of mine may sit one at your right hand and the other at your left in your kingdom." Jesus's answer provoked resentment between the two brothers as well as from the other disciples: "You do not know what you are asking. Can you drink the cup of suffering that I am going to drink? Are you prepared to do what I must do with thanksgiving? As for seats at my right hand and my left, these are not mine to grant; they belong to those to whom they have been allotted by my Father." (Matt 20:20–28)

When the other disciples heard this response, they became indignant with the two brothers. How dare they compare themselves to Jesus. The jealousies and resentments of the disciples were rebuked when Jesus said: "You know that among the gentiles the rulers lord it over them, and great men make their authority felt. Among you this is not to happen. No; anyone who wants to become great among you must be your servant, and anyone who wants to be first among you must be your slave, just as the Son of man came not to be served but to serve, and to give his life as a ransom for many."

We, like the sons of Zebedee, want to be near power and reflected glory. And if we cannot sit on the throne we at least want to sit very close to it. If we do not dare to ask for this privilege ourselves, we let someone close to us ask for it. Jesus's teaching here is a reminder of our temptation to be like God, and of our resentment for not always being first in line or highly privileged. If we cannot attain the first place, we'll settle for the second place in the kingdom. Those who perceive themselves worthy of first place but have to be content with second place can only look upward with resentment and downward with suspicion. And then, in this competitive and jealous place, neither God nor humanity can be served.

When you cling to your complaints, your heart is full of resentment, and there is no room for God to enter and set you free. Resentment curtails the movements of the Spirit and diminishes the kingdom within. It replaces faith, hope, and charity with fear, doubt, and rivalry. It makes an enormous difference in our personal and communal lives whether we respond to life in anger and resentment, or in love and gratitude.

WHAT IS GRATITUDE?

The opposite of resentment is *gratitude* (from the Latin *gratia* = favor). Gratitude is more than an occasional "thanks be to God." Gratitude is the attitude that enables us to let go of anger, receive the hidden gifts of those we want to serve, and make these gifts visible to the community as a source of celebration.

Gratitude is at the heart of celebration and ministry.

When I think about what it means to live and act in the name of Jesus, I realize that what I have to offer to others is not my intelligence, skill, power, influence, or connections, but my own human brokenness, through which the love of God can manifest itself. Ministry is entering with our human brokenness into communion with others and speaking a word of hope. The great paradox of ministry is that when we minister in our weakness, we receive from those to whom we go. The more in touch we are with our own need for healing and salvation, the more open we are to receiving in gratitude what others have to offer us.

When I was studying Spanish in Cochabamba, Bolivia, I met Lucha, one of the maids working in the Instituto de Idiomas. We did not speak about God or religion, but her smile, her kindness, the way she corrected my Spanish, and her stories about her children created a sense of spiritual jealousy in me. I kept thinking: "I wish I had the purity of heart of this woman. I wish I could be as simple, open, and gentle as she is. I wish I could be as in touch." But then I realized that maybe she didn't know what she was giving me. Thus my ministry to her was to allow her to show me the Lord in her own gentle manner, and gratefully to acknowledge what I was receiving.

True liberation is freeing people from the bonds that have prevented them from giving their gifts to others. This is true not only for individual people but also—particularly—for certain ethnic, cultural, or marginalized groups. What does mission to the Indians or Bolivians or disabled persons really mean? Isn't it foremost to discover with them their own deep religiosity, their profound faith in God's active presence in history, and their understanding of the mystery of nature that surrounds them?

It is hard for me to accept that the best I can do is probably not give but receive. By my receiving in a true and open way, those who give to me can become aware of their own gifts. After all, we come to recognize our own gifts in the eyes of those who receive them gratefully. Gratitude thus becomes the central virtue of a Christian. The Greek word *charis* means "gift" or "grace." And what else is the *Eucharistic* life but a life of gratitude?

MOVING FROM RESENTMENT TO GRATITUDE

Moving away from resentment requires moving toward something more life giving, and that something is the attitude of gratitude. Resentment blocks action; gratitude lets us move forward toward new possibilities. Resentment makes us cling to negative feelings; gratitude allows us to let go. Resentment makes us prisoners of our passions. Gratitude helps us to transcend our compulsions to follow our vocation. Resentment exhausts us by complicated jealousies and ambiguities, stirring up destructive desires for revenge. Gratitude takes our fatigue away and gives us new vitality and enthusiasm. Resentment entangles us in endless distractions, pulling us down to banal preoccupations. Gratitude anchors our deepest self beyond this world and allows us to be involved without losing ourselves.

How can we break through the chains of resentment and free ourselves from the passion that paralyzes us? Resentment has very deep roots in our human condition and is not easily cleared away. But once we confess our resentments within a safe and supportive faith community, we create space for forgiveness and freedom. When this happens, God's liberating grace is able to make all things new. We learn how to sing a new song and develop a new spirit of thanksgiving in which all of life can be received as a gift.

Spiritual formation is the way by which resentment can slowly be transformed into gratitude. Through the spiritual practice of letting go of jealousy and bitterness and forgiving and affirming others, we can make rivals into friends and competitors into companions on the way to true greatness. Servanthood might sound like a pious idea, but it really asks for the humble recognition that our life is not our own to be defended but a gift to be shared. All we have has been given to us. Our part is to be grateful and to give thanks.

How to move from resentment to gratitude is a question not just for individuals but for religious institutions and communities of faith to answer. Whereas the Church, as an institution, is often a breeding place for resentment, authentic Christian community occurs where there is fertile ground for gratitude to grow, for gifts to be received, and for blessings to be shared.[3] Such a place embodies the true nature and function of what we call *church,* no matter where it gathers or what name it bears.

Authentic Christian community nurtures the spirit of gratitude and service in the spiritual life. It does so by inviting us to give constant attention to the condition of our hearts, where we listen to the voice of God and respond with thanksgiving. It calls for an ongoing willingness to remove our defensive armor and create inner space where the Spirit of God can live. It requires courage to scrutinize our compulsive selves and to open our hearts to new ways of being. It forms us into receivers instead of takers, and helps us see the pain and suffering of the world not as disturbing interruptions, but as invitations for a change of heart.

I met an old priest who said to me: "I complained for too long that my work was constantly being interrupted, until I discovered that my interruptions were my work." It is sad that he discovered this so late in life. Resentment is exactly the complaint that life does not unfold the way we planned; that our many goals and projects are constantly interrupted by the events of the hour, the day, and the year; and that there is no choice other than to become the passive victim of random incidents and happenstance. The movement to gratitude involves the discovery that God is the God of history and that things are quietly and slowly unfolding as they should. My spiritual task is to learn to listen to all that is going on and trust that God's hand is guiding me. Then life is no longer a series of interruptions to my schedule and plans, but rather the patient and purposeful way by which God forms and leads me day by day. Gratitude makes the interruption into an invitation, and the occasion of complaint into a moment for contemplation.

AM I A ROCK OR A DANCER?

I once saw a stonecutter remove great pieces from a huge rock on which he was working. In my imagination I thought, *That rock must be hurting terribly. Why does this man wound the rock so much?* But as I looked longer, I saw the figure of a graceful dancer emerge gradually from the stone.

I have spent a good deal of my life building a stone wall of protection around my heart. Now, when I actually hear the truth about my hardness of heart, it seems as though one of the stones is being taken out of my protective wall. This wounds me and makes me frightened and angry. It's a big struggle. But I'm trying to be more aware and less fearful in the process. "Don't be so afraid," I hear the inner voice of love say to me. "Recognize everything in your life as a gift, and consciously give thanks. Make more room for joy in your life. Let the stones be taken away, and be grateful. Go beyond your comfort zone, and trust. Have courage, open yourself to your heart's deeper desire, and let the wall fall down. Open yourself, and allow me to remove your heart of stone and give you a heart of flesh."

Transfiguration from Pereslavl (c. 1403) by Theophan the Greek

The icon was created for the sole purpose of offering access to the inner sanctuary of prayer and bringing us close to the heart of God. For those who gaze on the visionary images, what is opaque becomes transparent; nature and time are transformed, and we ourselves can be transfigured. For God makes all things new.

—Henri Nouwen, "Prayer and Ministry"

Chapter 2. From Illusion to Prayer

The Bench at Saint-Remy (1889) by Vincent van Gogh

A carpenter and his apprentice were walking together through a large forest. When they came across a tall, huge, gnarled, old, beautiful tree, the carpenter asked his apprentice: "Do you know why this tree is so tall, so huge, so gnarled, so old and beautiful?" The apprentice looked at his master and said: "No . . . why?"

"Well," the carpenter said, "because it is useless. If it had been useful it would have been cut long ago and made into tables and chairs, but because it is useless it could grow so tall and so beautiful that you can sit in its shade and relax."

—adapted from Chuang Tzu, *The Inner Chapters*

Sunflowers (1889) by Vincent van Gogh

"Oh!" Vincent wrote to Theo, "those who don't believe in this sun ... are real infidels. The sun, light in the darkness, light that brightens nature and people, light that calls the dead from their graves. Those who have eyes to see will recognize that all light comes from the same sun."

—from Vincent van Gogh, *Letters to Theo*

Woman Dancing (1809–1812) by Antonio Canova

I once saw a stonecutter remove great pieces from a huge rock on which he was working. In my imagination I thought, *That rock must be hurting terribly. Why does this man wound the rock so much?* But as I looked longer, I saw the figure of a graceful dancer emerge gradually from the stone.

—Henri Nouwen, *Turn My Mourning into Dancing*

Chapter 5. From Fear to Love

Icon of the Old Testament Trinity (c. 1410) by Andrei Rublev

As we place ourselves in front of the icon in prayer, we come to experience a gentle invitation to participate in the intimate conversation that is taking place among the three divine angels and to join them around the table.

—Henri Nouwen, *Behold the Beauty of the Lord*

Chapter 6. From Exclusion to Inclusion

Allegory of the Transfiguration, in the apse of the
Basilica di Sant'Apollinare Nuovo, Ravenna, Italy (early Christian)

On the original cross of Jesus, we are told, the vertical and horizontal beams were of equal length. You can draw a perfect circle around the cross beams. The horizontal beam points left toward the Jewish people, the right toward the Gentiles. The vertical beam points toward God above and to the earth below. This is the mystery and promise of the Cross—the cross beams grounded on the mountain where Jesus brings all divergent points together into one circle of God's great love.
—Henri Nouwen, "Our Story, Our Wisdom"

Chapter 6. From Exclusion to Inclusion

Wheel artwork by Francis Maurice, Tracy Westerby, and
Amanda Wittington-Ingram, members of L'Arche Daybreak in
Richmond Hill, Ontario, Canada

I have always been fascinated by these wagon wheels with their wide rims,
strong wooden spokes, and big hubs. These wheels help me understand
the importance of a life lived from the center. When I move along the rim,
I can reach one spoke after the other, but when I stay at the hub, I am in
touch with all the spokes at once.

—Henri Nouwen, *Here and Now*

Old Man in Sorrow (1890) by Vincent van Gogh

The old man is "worn out," Vincent notes, "on the threshold of eternity." In this print "I have tried to express . . . the existence of God and eternity—in the infinitely touching expression of such a little old man, of which he himself is perhaps unconscious, when he is sitting quietly in his corner by the fire."

—from Vincent van Gogh, *Letters to Theo*

In spiritual formation, you may think about your life as a strong rock wall, resisting anyone and anything that tries to change it. Resentment makes us blind to God's carving hand, but gratitude helps us recognize the process—that slowly but surely, we are being formed into a beautiful work of art; that we are being prepared to be a person who can offer our own pains as a source of healing for others. In real formation, God is allowed to carve into the rock of our soul and pull out any stones of resentment. Every time a stone rolls out, small *or* large, it hurts a little or a lot. Every time we have to give up a familiar passion or favorite concept, a precious idea or definitive plan for our life, a justifiable attitude or habitual behavior, and especially a treasured friendship or community, we feel an inner protest. But when we are willing to see God's caressing hand at work, we might discover that after much carving we have an empty place where we may be filled and healed and finally transformed into the grateful dancer God intends for us to be.

To be healed of resentment and move into gratitude requires me to dance—to believe again, even amid my pain, that God will orchestrate and guide my life. The mystery of the dance is that its movements are discovered in taking the steps one by one: Some slow, some quick. Some smooth, some not. If all steps on the journey are movements of grace, we can be grateful for every moment we have lived, knowing that *all is grace.*

ALL IS GRACE

Gratitude at its deepest level embraces *all* of life with thanksgiving: the good and the bad, the joyful and the painful, the holy and the not so holy. Jesus calls us to recognize that gladness and sadness are never separate, that joy and sorrow really belong together, and that mourning and dancing are part of the same movement. That is why Jesus calls us to be grateful for every moment that we have lived and to claim our unique journey as God's way to mold our hearts to greater conformity with God's own.

Gratitude is not a simple emotion or an obvious attitude. It is a difficult discipline in which I constantly reclaim my whole past as the concrete way God has led me to this moment and is sending me into the future. It is hard precisely because it challenges me to face my painful moments—experiences of rejection and abandonment, feelings of loss and failure—and gradually to discover in them the pruning hands of God purifying my heart for deeper love, stronger hope, and broader faith.

I am gradually learning that the call to gratitude asks us to say, "Everything is grace." Whether there is suffering or joy, I can say, "Yes, I want to live this, and I want to discover in this more fully the gift of life." When our gratitude for the past is only partial, our hope for a new future can never be full. As long as we remain resentful about things that we wish had not happened, about relationships that we wish had turned out differently, about mistakes we wish we had not made, part of our heart remains isolated, unable to bear fruit in the new life ahead of us. To reclaim our history in its totality means that we no longer relate to our past as years in which only good times can be remembered and bad times need to be forgotten, but as opportunities for an ongoing conversion of heart. In a converted heart all our past can be gathered up in gratitude, be remembered with joy, and become the source of energy that moves us toward the future.

We also need to remind each other that the cup of sorrow is also the cup of joy we share, and that precisely what causes us sadness can become the fertile ground for gladness when we recognize the *charis* in it. Let us not be afraid to look at everything that has brought us to where we are now, receive it with gratitude, and see it in the light of a loving God who guides us day by day.

GOING DEEPER:
EXERCISES FOR
SPIRITUAL FORMATION

Earlier in this chapter, Henri Nouwen told the sad story of resentful seminarians on a spiritual retreat where the Eucharist could not be *thanksgiving* because resentment cannot be celebrated. Given how destructive the passion of resentment can be in human life, the movement from resentment to gratitude is necessary. Once we enter into this movement of the Spirit, we can let go of our resentments and stretch out our arms to the God who sets us free for joyful service—service not as a religious obligation, but as a manifestation of our inner gratitude. Nouwen's challenge is for us to look at everything that has brought us to where we are now in the light of a loving and guiding God.

REFLECT AND JOURNAL

1. Can you name one difficult stepping-stone that has brought you to where you are now, and reflect on it in the light of a loving God who guides your steps?

2. For Nouwen, to be grateful means to live life as a gift— that wherever I live, whatever I do, or whatever happens to me, I see somewhere in the experience a gift for which to

be thankful. What past experiences in your life that were hard at the time can you now be truly grateful for?

3. The Apostle Paul encourages us to "give thanks always and for everything" (Eph. 5:20). Further, Paul reminds believers that "in all things God works for the good" (Rom. 8:28). In your journal, write down ten things that you can be thankful for today. Share these with your small group.

4. Read the parable of the lost sons in Luke 15:11–32. Write a page in your journal on the question, In what ways am I the older son in the parable? For further reading and reflection, see chapters 4 and 5 in Nouwen's *Return of the Prodigal Son,* or read part 2 of Nouwen's *Home Tonight* (see "For Further Reading" at the end of this book).

VISIO DIVINA: THE GRACEFUL DANCER

Russian troops entered Paris in 1815 with force and violence. In the aftermath of destruction and loss, an important acquisition was made for the Hermitage. Alexander I arranged for the purchase by private treaty of a collection of artworks belonging to Empress Josephine, former wife of Napoleon, housed in her Malmaison Palace. Among the priceless additions were four sculptures by Antonio Canova: *Hebe, Paris, Woman Dancing* (see *Woman Dancing* in the color insert), and *Cupid and Psyche.* As you ponder the *Dancer* image, reflect on the following insight of Nouwen's:

"I once saw a stonecutter remove great pieces from a huge rock on which he was working. In my imagination I thought, *That rock must be hurting terribly. Why does this man wound the rock so much?* But as I looked longer, I saw the figure of a graceful dancer emerge gradually from the stone."[4]

In what ways do you feel the pain of the rock being made into a statue of a dancer? What chipping away at the protective wall of your soul do you feel God may be engaged in right now? In what ways are you resisting or resenting the process? In what ways are you open or grateful? As you look at *Woman Dancing* by Antonio Canova, can you feel the cold marble of the statue? Can you sense the movements of the dancer in motion? Can you see yourself alone or with another on the dance floor? What would it take to make you dance with joy?

FIVE

From Fear to Love

~ The Fearful Hoarders ~

Once there was a group of people who surveyed the resources of the world and said to each other: "How can we be sure that we have enough in hard times? We want to survive whatever happens. Let us start collecting food and knowledge so that we are safe and secure when a crisis occurs." So they started hoarding, so much and so eagerly that other people protested and said: "You have much more than you need, while we don't have enough to survive. Give us part of your wealth!" But the fearful hoarders said: "No, no, we need to keep this in case of an emergency, in case things go bad for us too, in case our lives are threatened." But the others said: "We are dying now; please give us food and materials and knowledge to survive. We can't wait, we need it now!" Then the fearful hoarders became even more fearful, since they became afraid that the poor and hungry would attack them. So they said to one another: "Let us build walls around our wealth so that no stranger can take it from us." They started erecting walls so high that they could not even see anymore whether there were enemies outside the walls or not! As their fear increased they told each other: "Our enemies have become so numerous that they may be able to tear down our walls. Our walls are not strong enough to keep them away. We need to put explosives and barbed wire on top of the walls so that nobody will dare to even come close to us." But instead of feeling safe and secure behind their armed walls they found themselves trapped in the prison they had built with their own fear.

—Henri Nouwen, Presbyterian Peace Fellowship Breakfast address[1]

WHY ARE WE SO AFRAID?

The more people I come to know and the more I come to know people, the more I am overwhelmed by the negative power of fear. It often seems that fear has so invaded every part of our lives that we no longer know what a life without fear would feel like. Fear pervades our bodies, individually and communally. So many people let their thinking, speaking, and acting be motivated by fear. We fear for ourselves and fear for our neighbors. We fear that something terrible may happen.

There always seems to be something to fear: Something within us or around us. Something close or far away, something visible or invisible, something in ourselves, in others, or in God. When we think, talk, act, or react, fear always seems to be there: an omnipresent force that we cannot shake off. Often fear has penetrated our inner selves so deeply that it controls, whether we are aware of it or not, most of our choices and decisions. Untamed fear can become a cruel tyrant who takes possession of us and forces us to live as hostages in this house of fear.

When fear pervades our lives, we are living in the house of fear, and from there we look out on the world. What we see from that perch of fear is alienation and scarcity. Those with power and influence often use fear to foster inner tension and divide us from one another. Those who can make us afraid can also make us do what they want us to do. Fear is one of the most effective weapons in the hands of those who seek to control us: a father, a mother, a teacher, a doctor, a boss, a bishop, a church, or God. As long as we are kept in fear we can be made to act, speak, and even think as slaves.

The agenda of our world—the issues and items that fill newspapers and newscasts—are the agenda of fear and power. What am I going to do if I do not find a spouse, a house, a job, a friend, a benefactor? What am I going to do if they fire me, if I get sick, if an accident happens, if I lose my friends, if my marriage does not work out, if a war breaks out? But here is the spiritual truth about these fearful questions: they never lead to love-filled answers; underneath every fearful question many other fearful questions are hidden. Once I have decided that in order to have a child I must be able to offer that child a college education, I get caught in many new, anxious questions involving my job, the place I live, the friends I make, and so on. Once I conclude that I cannot be happy without influential friends and money, I will remain anxious and wanting more. Thus, fear engenders fear. It never gives birth to love.

The control that fear exerts on our lives may be subtle. We may not believe consciously that everyone around us is our enemy, but we behave as if that were true. When this is our day-to-day reality, we may one day realize that we have become strangers in our own land: fearful, isolated, and powerless. Instead of self-confidence and freedom, we experience anxiety and paralysis. Instead of hope and joy, we feel an inner emptiness and sadness. Instead of living in the house of love, where God dwells, we are living in the house of fear.

THE HOUSE THAT LOVE BUILT

When I was in Latin America among poor and oppressed people for several months, I observed those I lived with and slowly realized that they were not a fearful people. They were a simple and grateful people who lived in a fearful land. Where I saw hunger, suffering, and agony, I also found joy, gratitude, and peace.[2] Soon I realized that the other side of oppression, the other side of poverty in the Southern Hemisphere, is the fear, anguish, and captivity of those who live in the North. Somehow these two realities cannot be separated. Our suffering, caused by fearful hoarding and a lack of freedom, is not separated from the suffering and oppression of those who live in countries we call the "developing world." Somehow in North America we've nearly forgotten what leads to a life of love. We've almost sold out our collective hopes of dwelling in God's house of love for secured borders, security systems, and gated communities.

When St. John so beautifully says that *perfect love drives out fear*, he points to a divine love that comes from God. He does not detail a strategic plan with development goals or security systems. He does not speak about human affection, psychological compatibility, mutual attraction, or deep interpersonal feelings. All of that has its value, but the perfect love about which St. John speaks embraces and transcends all plans, feelings, emotions, and passions. The perfect love that drives out all fear is the divine love in which we are invited to participate as we learn to dwell in intimacy with the author of love. That intimate place of true belonging is therefore not a place made by human hands. It is fashioned for us by God, who came to pitch his tent among us, invited us to dwell in his place, and has prepared a room for us in his own house.

DWELLING IN LOVE

Various words for "home" are often used in the Old and New Testaments. The Psalms are filled with a yearning to dwell in the house of God, to take refuge under God's wings, and to find protection in God's holy temple; they praise God's holy place, God's wonderful tent, God's firm refuge. We might even say that "to dwell in God's house" summarizes all the aspirations expressed in these inspired prayers. It is therefore highly significant that St. John describes Jesus as the Word of God dwelling among us (John 1:14). Not only does John tell us that Jesus invites him and his brother Andrew to stay in his home (John 1:38–39); he also shows how Jesus gradually reveals that he himself is the new temple (John 2:19). This is most fully expressed in the farewell address, where Jesus reveals himself as our true home: "Make your home in me, as I make mine in you" (John 15:4). Jesus, in whom the fullness of God dwells, has become our home. By making his home in us he allows us to make our home in him. By entering into the intimacy of our innermost self he offers us the opportunity to enter into his own intimacy with God. By choosing us as *his* preferred dwelling place he invites us to choose him as *our* preferred dwelling place. We may wonder, Is it possible to live in the house of love, or are we so accustomed to living in fear that we have become deaf to the voice that says, "Do not be afraid"?

DON'T BE AFRAID

We are not alone in needing to learn to hear that voice. "Have no fear!" resounds throughout the New Testament. Angels, when they appear, always say, "Don't be afraid." This word was heard by Zechariah when Gabriel, the angel of the Lord, appeared to him in the temple and told him that his wife, Elizabeth, would bear a son; this voice was heard by Mary when the same angel entered her house in Nazareth and announced that she would conceive, bear a child, and name him Jesus.

By his life and ministry Jesus taught his disciples not to give in to fear. When the disciples were afraid of the great storm on the lake, Jesus was asleep in the boat! Like those early disciples, whenever the fear becomes overwhelming, we want to wake him up, anxiously saying: "Save us, Lord, we are going down." He says: "Why are you so frightened, you people of little faith?" Then he rebukes the winds and sea and makes all calm again (see Matt. 8:23–27). This voice was also heard by the women who came to the tomb and saw that the stone was rolled away: "Do not be afraid, do not be afraid, do not be afraid."

This is what the Lord says when he appears to the disciples in the Upper Room after the Resurrection: "Take heart, it is I; do not be afraid" (Matt. 28:10). "I am the Lord of love, who invites you to receive, to receive gifts of joy and peace and gratitude, and to let go of your fears so that you can start sharing what you are so afraid to let go of." The invitation of Christ is the invitation to move out of the house of fear and into the house of love: to move out of that place of imprisonment and into that place of freedom: "Come to me, come into my house, the house of love."

The reassuring voice, which repeats over and over again, "Do not be afraid, have no fear," is the voice we most need to hear. The voice uttering these words—*fear not!*—sounds all through history as the voice of God's messengers, be they angels or saints, and of Christ himself. It is the voice that announces a whole new way of being—a way of living in the house of love, the house of the Lord.

As Jesus travels with us in life, he teaches us how to return to the house of love. It is far from easy to grasp his teaching because we are driven to panic by looking at the impossible task, the high walls, the powerful waves, the heavy winds, and the roaring storm. We keep saying: "Yes, yes . . . but look!" Jesus is a very patient teacher. He never stops telling us where to make our true home, what to look for, and how to live. When we are distracted, we focus upon all the dangers and forget what we have heard. But Jesus says over and over again: "Make your home in me, as I make mine in you. Whoever remains in me, with me in them, bears fruit in plenty. . . . I have told you this so that my own joy may be in you, and your joy may be complete" (John 15:4, 5, 11). Thus, Jesus invites us to live in his house of love.

MOVING FROM FEAR TO LOVE

Prayer is the way out of the house of fear and into the house of love. Prayer helps us overcome the fear that is related to building our life just on the interpersonal—"What does he or she think of me? Who is my friend? Who is my enemy? Whom do I like? Dislike? Who rewards me? Punishes me? Says good things about me? Or doesn't?" We are concerned about personal identity and distinctions from others. As long as our sense of self depends on what other people think about us and say about us, and on how they respond to us, we become prisoners of the interpersonal, of that interlocking of people, of clinging to each other in a search for identity; we are no longer free but fearful.

One way to pray in a fear-filled world is to choose love over anxiety, to open the door of the heart to dwell in the intimate presence of the One who loves us. When we begin to understand at a deep, spiritual level that we live surrounded by love and in communion with God no matter what the external circumstances, we can let go of the fear that lurks on the outskirts of our minds. Hardly a day passes in our lives without an experience of inner or outer fears, anxieties, apprehensions, and preoccupations. But we do not have to live in fear. Love is stronger than fear: "There is no fear in love; but perfect love casts out fear" (1 John 4:18).

Never have I seen what it means to dwell in the house of love more beautifully depicted than in the icon of the Holy Trinity painted by Andrei Rublev in 1410 in memory of the great Russian saint Sergius (1313–92). This icon has been a helpful visual window into the house of love for me. The story behind it opens it up even more. (See color insert.)

Long ago in Russia, there were many attacks made on a small town, and in a monastery the monks got very nervous and could no longer concentrate on their prayers because of all the violent conflicts throughout the town. The abbot called his icon painter, Rublev, to paint an icon to help the monks remain prayerful in the midst of restlessness, trouble, and anxiety. Rublev painted an icon based on the visit of the three angels to Abraham in Genesis, seated around a table of hospitality. In the icon, the figure in the center points with two fingers to the chalice and inclines toward the figure on the left, who offers a blessing. A third figure on the right points to a rectangular opening on the front of the table through which the viewer is invited to enter and participate in the spiritual actions. Together, the three figures form a mysterious circle of movement in perfect proportion. So when the monks prayed with the icon and focused on that circle of hospitality, love, and intimacy, they realized that they did not have to be afraid. When they allowed themselves to be part of the community formed by the three figures and let themselves be drawn into that circle of safety and love, they were able to pray and not lose heart.

For me, praying with this icon, releasing my fears as I focus on that little doorway in the icon that leads to where God dwells in intimacy, hospitality, and welcome, has increasingly become for me a way to enter more deeply into the mystery of divine life while remaining fully engaged in the struggles of our hate- and fear-filled world.

DWELLING DAILY IN THE HOUSE OF LOVE

The challenge is to let go of fear and claim the deeper truth of who I am. When you forget your true identity as a beloved child of God, you lose your way in life. You become scared and start doing things not freely, but because of fear. But when you make space for God in your life and begin to listen to God's loving voice, you suddenly start to realize perfect love. You can claim it, and you can gradually let go of your fear. The fear may come back tomorrow and you will have to struggle, and you can again return from fear to love. Every time you feel afraid, you can open yourself to God's presence, hear God's voice again, and be brought back to perfect love that casts out fear and brings in greater freedom.

Yes, it is possible *not* to belong to the dark powers, *not* to build our dwelling place among them, but to choose the house of love as our true home. This choice is made not just once and for all but by intentionally living a spiritual life—praying at all times, practicing *lectio divina*, and breathing God's breath each moment. These spiritual practices and other disciplines remind us that we are the Beloved. The classical disciplines are hospitality, spiritual friendship, contemplative prayer, community forgiveness, and the celebration of life. Through regular spiritual practice we gradually move from the house of fear to the house of love.[3] And as the psalmist proclaimed, we can "dwell in the house of the Lord forever" (Ps. 23:6).

A HOUSE OF LOVE FOR ALL PEOPLE

Moving from the house of fear to the house of love is necessary not just for each of us individually, but for the survival of the human family. If we continue to focus on our many fears—our fear of terrorists, our fear of socialism, our fear of no longer being the strongest and wealthiest nation on earth, and many smaller fears—to justify spending more time, money, and energy to build more devastating weapons, our planet will have little chance of surviving past our lifetimes. We *must* move out of the place of death wishes and death threats and search as nations for ways toward international reconciliation, cooperation, and care. We need academies of peace, ministries of peace, and peacekeeping forces. We need educational reform, church reform, market reform, and even entertainment reform that make peace its main concern. We need a new economic order beyond capitalism and socialism that makes peace and justice its entire goal. We need to believe as nations that a new international order is possible, and that the rivalries between countries or blocs are as outdated as the medieval rivalries between cities.

Can we develop a global spirituality in which the demands of the gospel guide not only the behavior of individuals but that of nations as well? Is a mass movement possible leading from fear to love, from death to life, from stagnation to rebirth, from living as rivals to living as people of God who belong to one human family? Many will consider this grand vision naive. They are glad to accept the teachings of Jesus for their personal and family lives, but when it comes to international affairs they consider these same teachings unrealistic and utopian. Yet, Jesus sent out his apostles to make disciples not just of individual people but of all the nations and to teach these nations to observe his commandments (Matt. 28:19–20). At the last day, Jesus will call these same nations before the throne and raise the critical question: "What have you done for the least of mine?" (Matt. 2:31–46). Discipleship goes far beyond personal piety or communal loyalty. Whole nations, not just individuals, are called to leave the house of fear, where suspicion, hatred, and war rule, and enter the house of love, where reconciliation, healing, and peace can reign.

The great spiritual leaders, from St. Benedict to St. Catherine of Siena to Martin Luther King Jr. to Thomas Merton, have all grasped this truth: the power of the renewing Word of God cannot be kept within the safe boundaries of the personal and interpersonal. They call for a New Jerusalem, a new earth, a new global community. Those who dare to join in the circle of God's intimacy and hospitality are the new St. Francises of our time. They offer a glimpse of a new order that is being born out of the ruin of the old. The world is waiting for new saints—prophetic women and men who are so deeply rooted in the love of God that they are free to envision and create a new world where justice reigns and war is no more, where the old order of things has passed away. We yearn for the day when we shall dwell in love not just in moments free from fear, but fully and freely, forever.[4]

The house of the Lord is the house of love for all people. There is a circle of safety, intimacy, and hospitality in the house of love. In that house we can slowly let go of our fear and learn to trust. In that house we can find freedom, community, and joy. Peacemaking is possible when we live in the house of love. Justice can be practiced when we live in the house of love. Ministry is effective when we live in the house of love. There we can be, and move, and trust and love in freedom and without fear.

GOING DEEPER:
EXERCISES FOR
SPIRITUAL FORMATION

We hardly need reminding that the world is a dangerous place. We may be surrounded by people interested only in our destruction. We may live in enemy-occupied territory. We may be afraid of too many changes and all that is happening to our world. It may seem that the "principalities and powers" that rule the darkness of this age (Eph. 6:12) have invaded the structures of our society to such an extent that peace and justice are impossible to attain. We do not want to be afraid of people on the street, but we are. We do not want to lock our car, bike, or house over and over again, but we do. We do not like to warn our parents, children, and friends not to go out on the streets alone, but we do. In a world like ours, how do we move from fear to love?[5]

REFLECT AND JOURNAL

Here are some simple questions for private reflection or small-group discussion:

1. What causes you fear and anxiety today?

2. Of what or of whom are you most afraid?

3. What do you hoard or cling to out of the fear of scarcity?

4. When have you felt most safe and unafraid? What were the circumstances?

5. How has God shown love and care for you today?

6. What does the following verse mean to you: "Perfect love casts out fear" (1 John 4:18)?

VISIO DIVINA: LIVING IN THE HOUSE OF LOVE

Clear an extended time for visual prayer—at least ten minutes.[6] Look long and hard at Rublev's icon of the Holy Trinity. (See color insert.) Listen to what Nouwen says about the icon in *Behold the Beauty of the Lord:* "As we place ourselves in front of the icon in prayer, we come to experience a gentle invitation to participate in the intimate conversation that is taking place among the three divine angels and to join them around the table. The movement from the Father toward the Son and the movement of both Son and Spirit toward the Father become a movement in which the one who prays is lifted up and held secure."[7]

Trace with your eyes the circle of intimacy created by the three figures in the painting. Then fix your eyes on the small rectangular door on the front of the table. Every few moments, take your eyes from the icon and pray one of the phrases below aloud. Return your gaze to the icon. Reenter the circle of intimacy.

Prayerfully focus on the truth of one of these scripture verses or affirmations:

"The Lord is my refuge and strength, a very present help in trouble" (Ps. 46:1).

"In you, O Lord, I trust. I let go of my fears" (Ps. 31:14).

"For you are our God, and we are the people of your pasture" (Ps. 95:7).

"I am certain of this: neither death nor life, nor angels, nor principalities, nothing already in existence and nothing still to come, nor any power, nor the heights nor the depths, nor any created thing whatever, will be able to come between us and the love of God, known to us in Christ Jesus" (Rom. 8:38–39).

"Surely goodness and mercy shall follow me all the days of my life, and I shall dwell in the house of the Lord—the house of the Lord—forever" (Ps. 23:6).

At the end of your prayer time, repeat the following Psalm aloud:

There is one thing I ask of the Lord;
for this I long:
To live in the house of the Lord
all the days of my life. . . .
For there God keeps me safe in God's tent.
In the day of evil God hides me.
In the shelter of God's tent on a rock
God sets me safe. . . .
And now my head shall be raised
Above my foes who surround me.
And I shall offer within God's tent
a sacrifice of joy. (Psalm 27:4, 5, 6)

PART THREE

Mature Movements

SIX

From Exclusion to Inclusion

~ The Monk and the Cripple ~

Going to town one day to sell some small articles, Abba
Agathon (one of the Desert Fathers) met a crippled man on
the roadside, paralyzed in his legs, who asked him where
he was going. Abba Agathon replied, "To town to sell some
things." The other said, "Do me the favor of carrying me
there." So he carried him to town. The crippled man said
to him, "Put me down where you sell your wares." He did
so. When he had sold an article, the man asked, "What did
you sell it for?" and he told him the price. The crippled man
said, "Buy me a cake," and the other bought it. When Abba
Agathon had sold a second article, the sick man asked,
"How much did you sell it for?" and he told him the price
of it. Then the other said, "Buy me this," and he bought
it. Having sold all his wares, Agathon was ready to leave.
The man said to him, "Are you going back?" and Agathon
replied, "Yes." Then the man said, "Do me the favor of

carrying me back to the place where you found me." Once more picking him up, he carried him back to that place. Then the crippled man said, "Agathon, you are filled with divine blessings, in heaven and on earth." Raising his eyes, Agathon saw no man; it was an angel of the Lord.

—*The Sayings of the Desert Fathers*[1]

The call to solidarity always moves us from exclusion to inclusion in order to embrace a greater mystery and a larger community. The movement from exclusive to inclusive community calls for *radical hospitality, spiritual intimacy,* and *open Communion* in the Body of Christ.

RADICAL HOSPITALITY

The writer of the letter to the Hebrews encourages us to practice hospitality to strangers, "for in so doing some have entertained angels without knowing it" (Heb. 13:2). Often it is difficult to love and include those who do not seem to fit our opinions of the righteous or meet our expectations of good behavior. At first I found the story of Agathon and the crippled man irritating. This tale clearly shows how a sick person uses his illness to manipulate a naive monk and take advantage of him. It proves that ministers need training so they won't become victims of the selfishness of others. How often have I been taken in by beggars of all sorts who knew my soft spot and did not hesitate to take advantage of it? If I really want to minister, I had better learn the difference between serving my neighbors and being exploited by them. A little study in the area of human motivation and need is in order.

Abba Agathon, however, does not think in this way. He does not have any great plans or projects. He is not thinking about helping the poor or sick. He simply is going to the market to sell some small articles, probably some baskets he has woven in his cell. He is a person without power or influence, and therefore without cares or worries and very little to lose. When he meets the crippled man, he does what he is asked to do, without judgment or expectation. He makes himself available to the man and is led (some would say misled) to a place he would rather not go.

Most of us would prefer to make distinctions between those in need and those with the power to meet human needs. Agathon's actions reveal the true nature of compassion and community. When our hearts are filled with prejudices, worries, and fears, there is little room for a stranger. Real hospitality is not exclusive but inclusive, requires a radical openness, and creates space for a wide range of human experience. Real ministers are powerless servants who offer the gifts of availability and hospitality. Real ministry is a "suffering with" another in a community of equals in the solidarity of powerlessness. Agathon was not a passive wanderer who simply went along with whatever happened to him on his journey, but a person of faith who was actively following a divine call. He was not without direction but guided by his Lord. Here we touch the mystery of ministry, and why Agathon was praised with the words: "You are filled with divine blessings, in heaven and on earth."

ROAD TO DAYBREAK

Unlike Agathon, I wandered aimlessly for many years in universities, monasteries, and missions, trying to discern my true vocation and find a place I could call home. When I met Jean Vanier, the founder of L'Arche,[2] he saw right through me. He perceived that I was not very happy, but rather restless and anxious, looking for something I had not yet found. "Maybe our people have a home for you," he said. "Maybe they have something to teach you, something that you really need." It took me a while to hear it. Finally, in 1986, I left the academic world and joined L'Arche

Daybreak in Canada. Since then, my life has been frighteningly different than what it was before. I have had to let go of all my previous notions of church and community, traditional understandings about who is in and who is not, and to empty myself of long-held opinions and judgments. But in return, I have found a home of deep joy and new purpose.

At Daybreak I met Adam. In him I encountered not only a person with severe physical and emotional challenges, but one who opened the door for me to the place where God dwells. In my friendship with and care of Adam, I heard God say: "Blessed are the poor"—not those who *work* for the poor, but blessed are the *poor*. "Henri, are you willing to become poor so that I can dwell with you, too?"

Adam taught me that community is shaped around the fellowship of the weak. Adam could not care for his physical needs; he could not talk, work, eat by himself, or drive a tractor. As Adam's assistant I lived with him in a household of five assistants and five community members. From an outside perspective, the assistants are strong and powerful, and the community members who have handicaps are weak and helpless. But from the inside perspective, Adam was the strong one because he helped us form community, love one another deeply, and forgive one another our idiosyncrasies. And because of Adam's needs, we came to grips with our own. Together, we are a community of the weak who practice hospitality, availability, and solidarity in powerful ways.

WHAT IS COMMUNITY?

In my earlier life, *community* meant a safe and familiar place of belonging, where those not like me simply were not present. I came from a Dutch Catholic family where it was clear who *we* were and who *they* were. *They* were all non-Catholics. *They* were nonbelievers. *They* got divorced, or were gay. While *we* were okay because we believed the right teachings and lived a moral life. My family, my community, my seminary, and my church felt very safe and secure because the patterns and expectations were so clearly defined.

Gradually, while I was teaching at Yale and Harvard, my fences (and defenses) began falling away. I learned from my students that God was greater than my Roman Catholic conceptions, and spiritual community broader than I had previously assumed. When I arrived at L'Arche, bang, bang, bang, my whole worldview crumbled.[3] It is a frightening thing when boundaries are pushed out and walls break down. How could the nonbeliever be more believing than the believer, the outsider wiser than the insider? How could those without resources have something valuable to share? Slowly, I came to realize that the differences between Catholic and Protestant, Christian and Buddhist, religious and secular were not the kind of differences I thought they were; that there was a deeper unity below the surface of distinction.

Over time I reconstructed my worldview in light of my new vision of community as a place of forgiveness and celebration, where we are more similar than different. I came to realize that the difference between people with disabilities and those with different abilities just wasn't there anymore; that I could love those with physical and intellectual challenges because I had my own set of disabilities. I could be close to people in pain because somehow they revealed my pain to me. No longer did I have to compare myself with others by carving out a little niche and distinguishing myself. I finally understood that the great spiritual call is not to be different from the other, but to be of the same substance and being as another, to be at one with others. Rather than wandering off to the periphery of life, where I might discover some small difference, I am called to go to the center, where I realize my solidarity with all human beings.

Thomas Merton came to this enlightenment on the corner of

4th and Walnut streets in Louisville, Kentucky, on March 19, 1958. He writes in his journal:

> . . . suddenly realized that I loved all the people and that none of them were, or could be totally alien to me. As if waking from a dream—the dream of separateness, of the "special" vocation to be different. My vocation does not really make me different from the rest or put me in a special category except artificially. . . . I am still a member of the human race—and what more glorious destiny is there, since the Word was made flesh and became, too, a member of the Human Race![4]

Merton's experience of liberation from the "illusory difference" between human beings was both a revelation and a relief, he says, "and such a joy to me that I almost laughed out loud. And I suppose my happiness could have taken form in the words: 'Thank God, thank God that I am like others, that I am only a man among others. . . . It is a glorious destination to be a member of the human race.'"[5]

There, in a momentary experience of solidarity with the whole human race, we, too, may witness many walls and boundaries come tumbling down, including distinctions between minister and layperson, caregiver and care receiver, client or helper, male or female, young or old, married or celibate, white or person of color, homosexual or heterosexual. We need not make comparisons and judgments about others: I am not like him or her or them, I am more, I am better, I am different from the others; on a deeper level, we can realize our common humanity. In the light of God's unconditional love and our own belovedness, we may experience our hearts expanding as if there are no limits. In the community of the heart, no one is excluded. We belong to the same spiritual family, where "nothing human is alien to me."[6]

SPIRITUAL INTIMACY IN THE BODY OF CHRIST

Christianity has a wonderful doctrine, a long-held and solid, essential belief called the Incarnation. The Gospel of John records: "In the beginning was the Word, and the Word was with God, and the Word was God. . . . The Word became flesh and dwelt among us" (John 1:1, 14). And St. Paul says: "For in Christ all the fullness of the Deity lives in bodily form and you have been given fullness in Christ, who is head over every power and authority" (Col. 2:9). The eternal God became human flesh in Jesus, son of Mary, and the Spirit of God is in us today as the Body of Christ. In the mystery of the Incarnation, the truth is revealed that the human body, and the spiritual intimacy of community as the Body of Christ, is the place where God is pleased to dwell (Col. 1:19).

Real spiritual life is an enfleshed life. In the Incarnation, Christ did not cling to his divinity but emptied himself and became human (Phil. 2). No longer is divine life found outside the body since God decided to become one of us. That's why St. Paul can say: "Do you not know that your body is a temple of the Holy Spirit, who is in you, whom you have received from God? You are not your own; you were bought at a price. Therefore honor God with your body" (1 Cor. 6:19–20).

When we realize that our bodies are the temple of the Holy Spirit, we can come together in community and experience a new dimension of physical and spiritual intimacy. God is in our midst, now and always. The Body of Christ is our true home. Long before we were born, we already had been seen, known, loved, and held safe in God's hands. We were bound together in God's heart long before we met each other here and now. Long before we could say to each other, "I need you, I love you, hold me, touch me, care for me," there was a Voice that said: "You are my beloved, on you my favor rests." Long before we learned to care for each other, we were cared for by our Creator: "Can a mother forget the baby at her breast and have no compassion on the child she has borne?" declares the Lord. "Though she may forget, I will not forget you! See, I have engraved you on the palms of my hands: your frame [i.e., body] is ever before me" (Isa. 49:16).

Out of the reality of our eternal belonging, we find each other in community. Out of that original intimacy, we express our love and affections. Out of the divine compassion, we offer and receive care. In our bodies no less than in our spirits, we long to reclaim that original place of blessing and to be held close, feel safe, and be made whole.

Human embodiment does present an earthly challenge to our restless bodies and souls. I confess that I have never felt completely at home in my body, and this is a scary thing for me to talk about. As a Christian and a celibate, I sometimes get resentful or judgmental when I encounter others who do not seem to share my convictions or value my commitments. I know that I need to be more comfortable in my own body in order to celebrate fully the way other people may be in theirs. Affirming the goodness and beauty of the body, mine and others, I have come to believe, is a spiritual activity. To be intimate with God I need to come home to my body, where God is pleased to dwell.

I am challenged by my community to claim a new freedom to love and accept others who may have different understandings of how to live a faithful and spiritual life. Rather than blame, judge, or compare, I can choose to accept, affirm, and celebrate another. Rather than avoiding persons who do not live the way I do or believe what I believe, I can learn to be with them in a personal, compassionate, and creative way. If I am rooted in my own spirit and comfortable in my own body, I will be less judgmental.

To embrace a universal and inclusive vision of community means that we are not to judge the motives and choices of others. "Judge not, that you be not judged," Jesus said (Matt. 7:1). One of the early desert fathers, Abba John, said to his monks, "Why don't you throw off the heavy burden and take the light burden?" The puzzled monks then asked, "What is the heavy burden and what is the light burden?" Abba John replied, "The heavy burden is judging other people, and the light burden is accepting the judgment of others."[7] Judging others is a heavy load; why not let it go? Being judged by others is a relatively light load; why worry about it? Often I have asked myself: What would it be like if I no longer had any desire to judge another? Or be controlled by the judgments of others? I would walk on the earth as a very light person indeed!

To come to that inner place of not judging in the face of the enormous variety of human experience and expressions is a long road of faith. To overcome that constant need to determine my comparative place, and to be simply who I am, can make me whole. To finally let go of that burden is one of the greatest joys and freedoms in life.

WHO IS WELCOME IN THE CIRCLE?

The Eucharist, for me, is the most tangible and physical way of celebrating God's inclusive love in the Body of Christ. When Jesus said to his disciples, "This is my body broken for you," he was speaking quite literally about his physical death as well as our embodied spiritual life. In our own flesh and blood, in our own bodies, we discover the *real presence* of the living Christ among us. Together, we "taste and see that the Lord is good." Through the spiritual act of eating simple bread and drinking hearty wine, we experience the mystery of the Incarnation. In the human touch, in the physical eating and drinking, and even in the dancing, we are made new. Who we truly are in the core of our being is expanded and energized with new physical strength and spiritual vitality. The very substance of our being is *transformed* (I hesitate to use the word *transubstantiated* since it is so often misunderstood) in participating in the mystery of the Eucharist.[8] When we eat and drink together, in the circle of God's love, we actually become the Body of Christ.

For many, the Eucharist has become a place of painful exclusion, empty ritual, or superstition. Yet it is our greatest spiritual gift and the physical place of prayer and healing. If there is anything I would like to know better, live deeper, celebrate more authentically, and call more people into, it is precisely the mystery of that real presence in the Word and Offering made visible in our midst. Jesus never said, "Munch and sip" the bread and wine. He said, "Eat me up, drink me empty, take it all in. Don't hold back. I want to become part of you. I want you to become part of me. I don't want to be separate anymore. I want to live within you, so that when you eat and drink, I disappear because I am within you. I want to make my home in you, and invite you to make your home in me." (See John 6:53–58.)

CONCLUSION: DRAW THE CIRCLE WIDE

As we recognize God's presence in our own hearts, we can also recognize the divine presence in the hearts of others. Where God dwells with me, I find all my sisters and brothers. To listen carefully to the voice of the One who calls us the "beloved" is to learn that that voice excludes no one. When we see only darkness within ourselves, we can see only darkness in others, but when we see the light of God within ourselves, we can see God's light in others. As the psalmist declares: "In God's light we see light" (Ps. 36:9).

Authentic community, like solitary prayer, is primarily a quality of the heart. Community can be lived well only if it comes out of communion with God. And in this community of faith, all are included, even those we think do not belong. To move from exclusive notions of Christian community to a more universal and inclusive vision of the human family of God is a difficult journey and requires a mature and confident faith. The God of all the nations is not just our private God. The God who dwells in our inner sanctuary is also the God who dwells in the inner sanctuary of each human being. Intimacy with God and solidarity with all people are two aspects of the indwelling presence of God. These two realities can never be separated. They come together in the physical place called the human body and are realized in community—the Body of Christ, celebrated in the Eucharist. Therefore, we can draw the circle wide.

GOING DEEPER:
EXERCISES FOR
SPIRITUAL FORMATION

REFLECT AND JOURNAL

Spiritual formation is an exercise not of private piety but of corporate spirituality. We do have personal experiences of spiritual formation, but together we are formed as the people of God. *Communion* with God, *community* with others, and *ministry* together can be envisioned as component parts of a wheel. Meditate for a moment on the metaphor of the wagon wheel as described by Nouwen in *Here and Now*:

> I have always been fascinated by these wagon wheels with their wide rims, strong wooden spokes, and big hubs. These wheels help me understand the importance of a life lived from the center. When I move along the rim, I can reach one spoke after the other, but when I stay at the hub, I am in touch with all the spokes at once.[9]

Draw a circle that represents your community of faith. Locate family members, friends, colleagues, and significant relationships either within or outside the circle. Think about who's in and who's out and why.

Pray for those who are inside your circle. Pray for those outside the circle.

What would it take to draw the circle wider?

VISIO DIVINA: THE CROSS AND THE CIRCLE

Can you visualize the cross of Jesus Christ within the circle of God's love?[10] (see color insert, *Allegory of the Transfiguration.*) On the original cross of Jesus, we are told, the vertical and horizontal beams were of equal length. You can draw a perfect circle around the crossbeams.[11] The horizontal beam points left toward the Jewish people, the right toward the Gentiles. The vertical beam points toward God above and to the earth below. This is the mystery and promise of the cross—the crossbeams grounded on the mountain where Jesus brings all divergent points together into one circle of God's great love.

Over the centuries Christians made the vertical beam longer and longer. Somewhere along the way a second crossbeam was added. The time has come to reclaim the cross with equal beams so that we can be an authentic community of faith that excludes no one. Jesus broke down the boundaries of time and place, and the barriers of race and culture that divide humanity. He became for all people the One who redeems that which has been broken and reconciles that which was divided. "For in Christ," says the scripture, "all the fullness of God dwells in bodily form. And through his life, death, resurrection, and ascension, God has reconciled all things, whether things on earth or things in heaven, having made peace through the blood of the cross" (Col. 19–20). That's why Jesus was able to say: "If I am lifted up from the earth, I will draw all people to myself" (John 12:32).

VISIO DIVINA: TURNING THE WHEEL

I like to think about the spiritual life as a big wagon wheel with a hub, a rim, and many spokes.[12] (See color insert, wheel artwork.) In the middle is the hub—the heart of God and the place of prayer. To pray is to move to the center of all life and all love. The hub reminds me of the importance of a life lived from the center. Often in ministry, it looks like we are running around the rim trying to reach everybody. But God says, "Start in the hub; live in the hub. Then we will be connected with all the spokes, and you won't have to run so fast." It's precisely in the hub, in that communion with God, that we discover the call to community. When I pray alone, I enter into my own heart and find there the heart of God, who speaks to me of a love for all. The closer I come to God, the closer I come to all my brothers and sisters in the human family. And I recognize that there, right there, is the place where all of my brothers and sisters are in communion with God and with one another. Solitude always calls us to community. Community is where solitude kisses solitude—where, as Rilke says, "[s]olitudes salute each other."[13] In solitary prayer, I realize I'm part of a human family, and that I want to be together and minister together with that family. By turning the wheel, I move from communion to community to ministry.

SEVEN

From Denying to Befriending Death

~ Twins in the Womb ~

Twins were talking to each other in their mother's womb. The sister said to the brother, "I believe there is life after birth." Her brother protested vehemently, "No, no, this is all there is. This is a dark and cozy place, and we have nothing else to do but to cling to the cord that feeds us." The little girl insisted, "There must be something more than this dark place. There must be something else, a place with light where there is freedom to move." Still she could not convince her twin brother.

After some silence, the sister said hesitantly, "I have something else to say, and I'm afraid you won't believe that, either, but I think there is a mother." Her brother became furious. "A mother!" he shouted. "What are you talking about? I have never seen a mother, and neither have you. Who put that idea in your head? As I told you, this place is all we have. Why do you always want more? This is not such a bad place, after all. We have all we need, so let's be content."

The sister was quite overwhelmed by her brother's response and for a while didn't dare say anything more. But she couldn't let go of her thoughts, and since she had only her twin brother to speak to, she finally said, "Don't you feel these squeezes every once in a while? They're quite unpleasant and sometimes even painful." "Yes," he answered. "What's special about that?" "Well," the sister said, "I think that these squeezes are there to get us ready for another place, much more beautiful than this, where we will see our mother face-to-face. Don't you think that's exciting?"

The brother didn't answer. He was fed up with the foolish talk of his sister and felt that the best thing would be simply to ignore her and hope that she would leave him alone.

—Henri Nouwen, *Our Greatest Gift*[1]

Death often happens suddenly—a car accident, a plane crash, a fatal fight, a war, a flood, and so on. When we feel healthy and full of energy, we do not think much about our death. Still, death might come at any moment. If we are fortunate enough to have time and enough self-awareness to prepare for our eventual death, many questions must be faced: In what ways am I denying my mortality? Why am I so afraid? Have I any unfinished business? Have I forgiven those who have hurt me and asked forgiveness from those I have hurt? When we are at peace with all the people who are part of our lives, our death might cause great grief, but it will not cause guilt or anger.

These questions began to rise in importance to me when my mother died. Six months after she died, as I journeyed through my grief, I wrote a letter of consolation to my father suggesting that it might be an opportune time for us both to confront our own deaths. "Ever since we saw her still face in the hospital," I remember writing him, "we have wondered what death really is. It is a question mother has left us with, and we want to face it, enter it, explore it, and let it grow in us. By so doing we may be able to console one another."[2] What I learned from grieving my mother's death and the deaths of others is that it is important to face death before we are in any real danger of dying and to reflect on our mortality before our conscious and unconscious energy is directed to the struggle to survive. If we start thinking about death only when we are terminally ill, our reflections will not give us the support we need as death draws near. As the German mystic Jakob Böhme once said: "Who dies not before he dies, is ruined when he dies."[3]

The story about twins in the womb helps us to think about death in a new way. Do we live as if this life is all we have, as if death is absurd and we had better not talk about it? Or do we choose to claim our divine childhood and trust that death is the painful but blessed passage that will bring us face-to-face with our God? When we are ready to die at any moment, we are also ready to live at any moment. For me, preparing for my own death involved befriending death, claiming my belovedness, becoming a child again, and trusting in the Communion of Saints. I invite you to make these movements, too.

BEFRIEND YOUR DEATH

I like the expression "to befriend death." I first heard it used by Jungian analyst James Hillman, who emphasized the importance of "befriending"—befriending your dreams, befriending your shadow, befriending your unconscious. He made it convincingly clear that in order to become full human beings, we have to claim the totality of our experience; we come to maturity by integrating not only the light but also the dark side of our story into our self-hood.[4] That made a lot of sense to me, since I am quite familiar with my own inclination, and that of others, to avoid, deny, or suppress the painful side of life—a tendency that always leads to physical, mental, or spiritual disaster. Befriending death seems to be the basis of all other forms of befriending. I have a deep sense that if we could move from denying to befriending our death before we die, if we could relate to death as a familiar guest instead of a threatening enemy, we would be freer of fear, guilt, and resentment.

How Do We Befriend Death?

I remember visiting a young man named Peter in a Toronto hospital who was suffering from AIDS and was going to die. His illness had rapidly progressed, and his hope for life had decreased. Here was a good man, a teacher, who had written and taught about spirituality and was loved by his many students. Peter was a man who deeply believed in the love of God and had dedicated his life to his vocation. Now he was thin and bald because of chemotherapy, and he was paralyzed from the cancer in his spine. Fr. Jan Laak and I were there—not for very long, actually—when something surprising happened in that room that made me see life and death a bit differently. Peter's partner, a beautiful man, said forcefully: "We are going to fight this! You are not going to die. We're going to win this battle, and we won't let death get the better of us." I really admired him. He spoke as the warrior who looked death in the face. He reminded me of Paul Monette, who wrote *Borrowed Time* about his partner, Roger Horwitz, who said, "I'm going to fight it. I'm going to win. We are not going to die."[5]

I then talked to Peter, and his was a different kind of voice. Peter said, "Why, Henri, why is this happening to me? I'm so angry at God for putting me here. I have dedicated my life to God, I have shared God's love with hundreds of people, and here I am dying at a young age. I can't take it. I don't want it. I don't even know how I got through this whole thing. I'm confused and angry and frustrated. I feel abandoned." His voice was the voice of resistance, of the protester. He was saying no to the suffering: "I don't want this and I am mad at God. I protest. I put up my fist and say, 'No!'" Peter was too weak to be the warrior, too anxious, too much in pain. But he cried out and said, in effect: "Let this cup pass me by. I don't want this. It's awful."

When I was walking home with Jan, I asked, "*What* is the way here? Is there any way that my friend and his partner can go one more step and embrace the truth of their reality? Can Peter befriend the evil twin of death that stands in his room and say, 'Yes, you have been my enemy, but I am called to love my enemy, and I want to love you. I want to embrace you. I want to be with you without fear.'" I kept thinking, "Why is it so hard for Peter to befriend death, and for his partner to make the same choice?" And then I knew. They were both saying that if we start embracing death, we will die sooner. If we start thinking about death, we are giving up the fight. If we allow death to come into our room and embrace us, we can no longer resist.

I don't believe that is true. Rather, I deeply believe that when we become lovers of life and death, when we embrace our enemy, when we befriend our mortality, we can become better warriors and stronger resisters through the power of love. I say this with some intimate knowledge of this truth.

A few years ago I was hit by a car and ended up in the hospital. I was feeling very uncomfortable lying on the gurney, but I didn't have any external injuries to speak of, so I thought I would be released to return home. When the doctor finally examined me, he was kind but clear, saying, "You might not live long. There is serious internal bleeding. We will try to operate, but we might not succeed." Suddenly everything changed. Death was right there in the room with me. I was shocked and scared, and there were many thoughts going through my mind when I realized that this might be the end of my life.

I did not feel ready to let go of my life and face my time of death. I felt I had unfinished business to take care of, unresolved anger and resentment, continuing conflicts with people with whom I live or had lived. A sense of not being forgiven, of not forgiving others, kept me clinging desperately to life. In my mind's eye, I saw the men and women who aroused within me feelings of anger, jealousy, and even hatred. By not truly forgiving them from the heart, I gave them a power over me that kept me chained to my wounded existence. In the face of death, I felt a deep desire to forgive and to be forgiven, to let go of all evaluations and opinions, and to be free from the burden of judgments. I felt an immense desire to gather around my bed all who were angry with me and all with whom I was angry, to embrace them, to ask them to forgive me, and to offer them my forgiveness.

In confronting death, I had a deeper experience than I had ever had before: a vision of pure and unconditional love. In the midst of my confusion and shock and unresolved guilt, I became very calm, very at rest, and there was an embrace of God that reassured me and gently told me, "Don't be afraid. You are safe. I am going to bring you home. You belong to me, and I belong to you." I hesitate to speak simply of Jesus, because of my concern that the name of Jesus might not evoke the full divine presence that I felt, inviting me to come closer and to let go of all fears. But when I walked around the portal of death, all ambiguity and uncertainty were gone. Jesus was there, the Lord of my life, saying, "Come to me, come."

I was so amazingly at peace that later that night after the surgery, when I woke up in the intensive care unit, I felt extremely disappointed. I asked myself, "What am I doing here, and why am I still alive?" I kept wondering what happened to me. Gradually I realized that perhaps for the first time in my life I had contemplated my death not through the eyes of fear but through the eyes of love. In befriending death, I was no longer afraid. Somehow, if only for a moment, I had known God. I could be in the world in a different way, as a warrior and as a resister, but motivated not by fear but by love. I had become a lover of life and death.[6]

RECLAIM YOUR BELOVEDNESS

Once we relate to death as a familiar friend instead of a threatening enemy, we will be able to shed many doubts and fears, face our mortality, and live in the freedom and knowledge that we are God's beloved sons and daughters. Though I have known this to be true for many years, I have to reclaim the truth of my belovedness from time to time.

Our fear of illness, death, and the future takes away our freedom and gives our society the power to manipulate us with threats and promises. When we reach beyond our fears to the One who loves us with an everlasting love, then oppression, persecution, and even death are unable to control us. All forms of evil, illness, and death lose their final power over us. We come to the deep inner knowledge—a knowledge of the heart more than of the mind—that we are born out of love and will die into love, that every part of our being is deeply rooted in love, and that nothing can separate us from this love of God, as the apostle Paul stated so beautifully:

> I am certain of this: neither death nor life, nor angels, nor principalities, nothing already in existence and nothing still to come, nor any power, nor the heights nor the depths, nor any created thing whatever, will be able to come between us and the love of God, known to us in Christ Jesus. (Rom. 8:38–39)

You can claim at any moment the deeper spiritual truth of who you are, even while everything around you suggests otherwise.

When life challenges your core identity or others try to define you differently, you can claim your truth, claim your journey, claim your family: "I am God's beloved!" It has to come right from your gut, right from your center, right from your heart. Listen to that voice, that incredible voice of love: "You are my beloved. On you my favor rests."

That's the voice that Jesus heard in the Jordan River confirming who he is. Jesus lived his life as the Beloved even when the demon said, "Prove it! Prove that you are the One by doing something relevant, by changing stones into bread. Prove that you are the Beloved by throwing yourself on the Temple so everyone can see how wonderful you are. Prove that you are the Beloved through power and influence so you can spread good news to people." Jesus rebuked the demon and said, "I don't want to prove anything. I *am* the Beloved because that's what the voice said at the Jordan River."

That same voice was heard again by Peter, James, and John in the light of Mount Tabor: "This is my Son, the Beloved; he enjoys my favor. Listen to him" (Matt. 17:1–8). I am convinced that the voice from heaven was not speaking just to Jesus or about Jesus. The voice also is speaking to us and about us. We, too, have been anointed as the beloved sons and daughters of God. Jesus came to share his divine nature and identity with us, and to impart his Christhood. The Spirit of Jesus now helps us claim this deeper truth.[7]

Just for a moment, in your prayer and meditation, try to enter this enormous mystery: that you, like Christ, are God's beloved child. In you, God is well pleased. Your belovedness precedes your birth. It will follow you all the days of your life and beyond death. You are fully loved of God before your father and mother, brother, sister, family, or church loved you or didn't love you, hurt you or helped you. You are fully loved because you belong to God for all eternity. That's the truth of your identity. That's who you are. And you can reclaim it at any moment.

If you believe that you are beloved before you were born, and will be beloved after you die, you can realize your mission in life. You are sent here just for a little bit—for twenty, thirty, forty, fifty, or sixty years. The time doesn't matter. You are sent into this world to help your brothers and sisters know that they are as beloved as you are and that we all belong together in God's family.

We are sent into this world to be people of reconciliation. We are sent to teach and heal, to break down the walls that divide people into different categories of value. Young, old, black, white, gay, straight—whatever divisions you can come up with—Serb, Croat, Muslim, Jew, Catholic, Protestant, Hindu, Buddhist—beyond all those distinctions that separate us, there is a greater unity. Out of that essential unity you can live and proclaim the truth that every human being belongs to God's heart, which beats from eternity to eternity. The mystery of God's love is that when you know in your heart that you are chosen and blessed, you also know that others are chosen and blessed, and you cannot do other than embrace all humanity as God's beloved. Precisely as we confront life and death in all its many facets, we can finally say to God: "I love you, too."

BECOME A CHILD AGAIN

When I turned sixty, the Daybreak community gave me a big party. More than one hundred people came together to celebrate. John Bloss, eager as always to play an active role, was there—full of good thoughts, but his disability making it painfully difficult for him to express those thoughts in words. Still, he loves to speak, especially when he has a captive audience. With everyone sitting in a large circle, Joe, the master of ceremonies, said, "Well, John, what do you have to say to Henri today?" John, who loves the theatrical, got up, put himself in the center of the circle, pointed to me, and began to search for words. "You . . . you . . . are," he said with a big grin on his face. "You . . . you . . . are . . . uh . . . uh . . ." Everyone looked at him with great expectation as he tried to get his words out while pointing ever more directly at me. "You . . . you . . . are . . . uh . . . uh . . ." And then, like an explosion, the words came out. "An old man!" Everybody burst out laughing, and John basked in the success of his performance.

That said it all. I had become "an old man. . . ."

It seems fair to say that people between the ages of one and thirty are considered young; those between thirty and sixty are considered middle-aged; and those past their sixtieth birthday are considered old. But when you yourself are suddenly sixty, you don't feel old. At least I didn't. Indeed, I somehow keep forgetting that I have become old and that young people regard me as an old man. It helps me to look at myself in a mirror once in a while and see both my mother and my father when they were sixty years old, and remember how I thought of them as old people.

Being an old man means growing closer to death. In the past, I often tried to figure out if I could still double the years I had lived. When I was twenty, I was sure that I would live at least another twenty years. When I was thirty, I trusted that I would easily reach sixty. When I was forty, I wondered if I would make it to eighty. And when I turned fifty, I realized that only a few make it to one hundred. But now, at sixty, I am sure that I have gone far past the halfway point and that my death is much closer to me than my birth.

Old men and old women must prepare for death. But how do we prepare ourselves well? For me, it involves becoming a child again—reclaiming my childhood. This might seem to be opposite to our natural desire to maintain maximum independence. Nevertheless, becoming a child—entering a second childhood— is essential to dying a good death. Jesus spoke about this second childhood when he said, "Unless you change and *become* like little children, you will never enter the Kingdom of Heaven" (Matt. 18:3).

What characterizes this second childhood in the light of eternity? It has to do with a new dependence on God and others. For the first twenty or so years of life, we depend on our parents, teachers, and friends. Forty years later, we again become increasingly dependent. The younger we are, the more people we need so that we may live; the older we become, the more people we again need just to live. Life is lived from dependence to dependence.

That's the mystery that God revealed to us through Jesus, whose life was a journey from the manger to the cross. Born in complete dependence on those who surrounded him, Jesus died on one level as the passive victim of other people's actions and decisions. His was a journey from a first to a second childhood. He came as a child and died as a child, and he lived his life so that we may claim and reclaim our own childhood, and thus make our death—as he did his—into a new birth. "Unless you become as a child again," Jesus said, "you cannot enter into God's kingdom." In the process of befriending death and reclaiming our belovedness, we can become a free and little child again.

As I shared earlier, I was blessed with an experience that made it clear to me that death can be embraced with childlike trust. Facing death during my car accident and operation allowed me to get in touch with my childhood as never before. Bound with straps on a table that looked like a cross, surrounded by masked figures, I experienced my complete dependence. Not only did I fully depend on the skills of an unknown medical team, but my life was dependent on God alone. I knew deeply that, whether or not I survived the surgery, I was being held like a child in God's safe embrace. At once, I knew that all human dependencies are embedded in a divine dependence that makes dying part of a greater way of living.

The experience was so real, so basic, and so all-pervasive that it radically changed my sense of self and affected profoundly my state of consciousness. When I faced my death, I felt one thing: I didn't want to be alone. Somehow I want to be assisted. I want someone to be my midwife into death. Just as I was not born alone, I hope I will not die alone. Knowing that I am a child of God brings an immense sense of security and freedom.

We all have good and bad expectations about when and how we will die. It will be good to have your husband or wife or partner there, good to have your mom or dad there, good to have your friends and family nearby, good to have a therapist or a pastor available. It's good to be not alone. But none of these spiritual midwives finally can give us the spiritual power to make that passage without fear. Only our trust in God and our participation in the Communion of Saints can bring us through to the other side.

TRUST IN GOD AND THE COMMUNION OF SAINTS

In the movement from denying to befriending death, my deepest conviction is that the Spirit of God and the Communion of Saints allow us to make the passage with faith and courage. "I believe in the Holy Spirit, the Holy Catholic Church, the Communion of Saints, the resurrection of the body, and life everlasting," we proclaim in the creeds. We especially need to reclaim the historic and spiritual doctrine of the Communion of Saints as we face death and dying.

During the Protestant Reformation, the Roman Catholic doctrine of the Communion of Saints was associated with selling "indulgences" to pray for the dead and with buying people out of purgatory.[8] As a result, the Reformers held that true Christians could not pray to the saints or for the dead. The dead were justified by God alone, their destination sealed, and no one could buy or pray them out of purgatory. As a result, many people stopped praying for the dead or believing in the saints, since they no longer were part of the living Church on earth. I talk to a lot of people today who want to pray for those who have died and who want to believe in the Communion of Saints but don't know how to believe. After the Reformation and Counter-Reformation, the churches lost a deep sense of spiritual community.[9]

At L'Arche Daybreak, where I live, we continue to pray for those in our community who have passed on. We celebrate their life and death. We think about them every day; we have their pictures on the wall. Finally, Laurie, Helen, and Morris, who died last year, and many others are all there. They continue to send their spirit and their love to me. They continue to tell me what life is about. The more I hold on to their memories, the more active they are in my heart and in my life. I need them to help me live my life, just as they needed me when they were with me. They continue to teach me something about who I am and where I am going, and to whom I belong.

CONCLUSION

The final movement in the spiritual life requires radical trust in the One who loved us before our birth and will be with us after death. This was Peter's message from his hospital bed in Toronto. This also is the truth I hear from Simon Peter in the Gospels as he sees Moses and Elijah with Jesus, clothed in radiant light, and hears a voice from heaven proclaim: "This is my Beloved; listen to him" (Matt. 17:1–8).

In this light, I encourage you to look into the face of the angel of death and say, "I am not afraid. I will befriend my death. I will become like a dependent child again. I believe in the Communion of Saints and the Life Everlasting. And I will trust in the God who calls me beloved."

Prayer

O Lord, when shall I die? I do not know and I hope it will not be soon. Not that I feel so attached to this life . . . but I feel so unprepared to face you. I feel that by letting me live a little longer, you reveal your patience, you give me yet another chance to convert myself, more time to purify my heart. Time is your gift to me. Amen.[10]

GOING DEEPER:
EXERCISES FOR
SPIRITUAL FORMATION

What did Jakob Böhme mean when he said: "Who dies not before he dies, is ruined when he dies"?[11]

Where and how do you want to die?[12]

How does this final movement—from denying to befriending death—anticipate and summarize all the other movements of the spiritual life.

MEDITATION: THE GIFT OF PEACE

During his stay in Chicago, where he was giving the opening address, "Befriending Death," at the National Catholic AIDS Network Conference in 1995 (the address on which this chapter is based), Henri Nouwen visited his friend Joseph Cardinal Bernardin in the hospital. The cardinal at that time was fighting a terminal illness. Henri shared his vision of "befriending death before you die." He encouraged his friend to live his struggle with cancer openly as a pastor to his congregation and to face the prospect of death in the knowledge of his belovedness. Cardinal Bernardin's reflection confirms the value of Henri's insight for himself personally as well as for the Church at large. The following excerpt is a personal narrative from Bernardin's book *The Gift of Peace.*

A very significant thing happened during the month of July last year. Father Henri Nouwen, a friend of mine for more than twenty-five years, paid me a visit. He had come to conference in the metropolitan area and asked if he could come to see me. I said, "By all means." We spent over an hour together, and he brought me one of his latest books, *Our Greatest Gift: A Meditation on Dying and Caring.* We talked about the book, and the main thing I remember is that he talked about the importance of looking on death as a friend rather than an enemy. While I had always taken such a view in terms of my faith, I needed to be reminded at the moment because I was rather exhausted from the radiation treatments. "Life's very simple," he said. "If you have fear and anxiety and you talk to a friend, then those fears and anxieties are minimized and could even disappear. If you see them as an enemy, then you go into a state of denial and try to get as far away as possible from them." He said, "People of faith, who believe that death is the transition from this life to life eternal, should see it as a friend."

This conversation was a great help to me. It removed some of my anxiety or fear about death. When Father Nouwen died suddenly of a heart attack on September 21 of this year at the age of 64, everyone was shocked. Yet, there is no doubt that he was prepared. He spent a lifetime teaching others how to live, and how to die.[13]

REFLECT AND JOURNAL

In light of Nouwen's teachings on the movement from denying to befriending death, read the scripture about the Transfiguration of

Jesus and reflect on the Light of Mount Tabor that was seen by those who climbed the mountain.

Lectio Divina: The Light of Mount Tabor

Six days later, Jesus took with him Peter and James and his brother John and led them up a high mountain by themselves. There in their presence he was transfigured: his face shone like the sun and his clothes became as dazzling as light. And suddenly Moses and Elijah appeared to them; they were talking with him. Then Peter spoke to Jesus. "Lord," he said, "it is wonderful for us to be here; if you want me to, I will make three shelters here, one for you, one for Moses and one for Elijah." He was still speaking when suddenly a bright cloud covered them with shadow, and suddenly from the cloud there came a voice which said, "This is my Son, the Beloved; he enjoys my favor. Listen to him." When they heard this, the disciples fell on their faces, overcome with fear. But Jesus came up and touched them, saying, "Stand up, do not be afraid." And when they raised their eyes they saw no one but Jesus.[14]

A Meditation on Mount Tabor

There, on the mountaintop, they saw Jesus transfigured before them. "His face shone like the sun and his clothes became as dazzling as light." The prophets Moses and Elijah appeared to them, and they did not know what to say. Peter offered to make three tents for Jesus, Moses, and Elijah. While he was speaking, a bright cloud covered them with its shadow, and from the cloud the Voice spoke: "This is my Son, the Beloved; he enjoys my favor. Listen to him" (Matt. 17:1–8).

"It is difficult to climb Mount Tabor," says Fr. Rodney DeMartini. "It is a difficult climb because to ascend the mountain means to leave solid ground, the old streets, and all the friends behind. To ascend the mountain means to be lightheaded, yet sure-footed. To ascend the mountain means grabbing on outcroppings and hoping, no, believing that they will hold. To climb the mountain means believing that there is a top and that there is the other side."

Transformation happens on the mountain: Olivet, the Mount of Olives. Calvary, the Mound of Skulls. Zion, the Shining City on a Hill. Every mountain has its shadowy crevices and its peaks of grand views. Tabor, the Mount of Transfiguration, presents a dance of shadow and radiance. It happens on the mountaintop, where the voice of God is heard. [15]

> Prepare to climb the mountain. Set aside enough time, and set your sights high. Embrace the silence and solitude. Quiet your faculties, and listen.

> Read the Gospel text slowly and deliberately three times, imagining yourself on the mountaintop with Peter, James, and John. What do you see? What do you hear? What do you feel when Jesus says, "Do not be afraid." What would it mean for you to be transformed by such an experience on the mountain? Finally, what does this passage say about facing your own mortality, death, and new life?

> Write a paragraph in your journal about what you see and hear on the mountaintop.

> Share what you wrote with your spiritual formation group, spiritual director, or soul friend.

VISIO DIVINA: ON THE THRESHOLD OF ETERNITY

In the village of Etten, in the Netherlands, Vincent van Gogh sketched a still life of a sick farmer seated near the fireplace with his head in his hands and his elbows on his knees.[16] (see color insert, *Old Man with His Head in His Hands*.) The old man is "worn out," Vincent notes, "on the threshold of eternity." In this print I have tried to express . . . the existence of God and eternity—in the infinitely touching expression of such a little old man, of which he himself is perhaps unconscious, when he is sitting quietly in his corner by the fire." Vincent's vision of death and new life is revealed in his letter to his brother, Theo, dated November 15, 1878. In it he writes: "It is a sad and very melancholy scene, which must strike everyone who knows and feels that we also have to pass one day through the valley of the shadow of death, and that we also will have our share of tears and white hairs. What lies beyond this is a great mystery that only God knows, but He has revealed absolutely through His word that there is a resurrection of the dead."

Quietly sit, perhaps by a fireplace, and contemplate "On the Threshold of Eternity." Let your reflection inform your prayer.

EPILOGUE

Journey Inward, Journey Outward

Editor's Note: The following text is adapted from a handout Nouwen wrote for his course on Spiritual Formation and the editor's class notes (Yale Divinity School, 1980).

Spiritual formation, to use the words of Elizabeth O'Connor, requires both a *journey inward* and a *journey outward*.[1] The journey inward is the journey to find the Christ dwelling within us. The journey outward is the journey to find the Christ dwelling among us and in the world. The journey inward calls for the disciplines of solitude, silence, prayer, meditation, contemplation, and attentiveness to the movements of our heart. The journey outward in community and mission calls for the disciplines of care, compassion, witness, outreach, healing, accountability, and attentiveness to the movement of other people's hearts. These two journeys belong together to strengthen each other and should never be separated.

The spiritual life presents opportunities to enter into the center of our existence and to become familiar with the complexities of our own inner life. As soon as we feel at home in our own house—discover the dark corners as well as the light spots, the closed doors as well as the drafty rooms—our confusion will disappear, anxiety lessen, and creative work become possible. The skills needed here are *discernment* and *articulation*. Those who can clearly discern and articulate the different movements of their inner lives, who can name the competing forces in their souls, confront their demons, and clarify their experiences do not have to remain victims of the process. Rather, they can slowly and confidently overcome the obstacles that prevent the Spirit from entering into the arena of struggle and create space for the One whose heart is greater than their own.

Only out of the prayerful place of solitude and introspection can we hope for community and ministry. The journey inward precedes the journey outward, and the chronology is important. Spiritually, we need to know our selves and God in order to know other people. We need to love our selves and God in order to love each other. Communion with God precedes community with others and ministry in the world. Once the inward journey has begun, we can move outwardly from solitude to community and ministry.

Both the inward and outward journeys are journeys of discernment and conversion. They are difficult journeys, and we are wise not to try to take these journeys alone. Whether we move inward or outward in our spiritual life, we are grounded in God, and guarded by God, who "is greater than our hearts and knows everything" (1 John 3:21).

Living a spiritual life calls for spiritual formation, spiritual direction, and spiritual discernment. Though they are concurrent realities in the spiritual life, it may be helpful to consider them individually. Having read this book on *spiritual formation,* you have taken the first step in the long journey of faith. You now may need a *spiritual director,* because the journey of the spiritual life calls not only for determination, but also for a special knowledge of the terrain to be crossed.[2] Under the guidance of a spiritual director, and with the accountability of a community of faith, you may want to learn the ways of *spiritual discernment*. Together, spiritual formation, spiritual direction, and spiritual discernment constitute a trilogy of sorts of the spiritual life.[3]

Appendix:
Nouwen's Place in
Spiritual Development Theory

By Michael J. Christensen

Henri J. M. Nouwen—Roman Catholic priest, pastoral psychologist, university professor, prolific spiritual writer—understood the spiritual life as a *journey*—a journey inward to the heart and a journey outward in community and mission. Further, he describes the *journey-inward, journey-outward* as a series of spiritual movements from *this* quality to *that*, from things that enslave and destroy to liberation and life. Psychodynamically as well as spiritually, we move back and forth, he says, "between different poles as our lives vacillate and are held in tension."[1]

Spiritual formation, according to Nouwen, occurs as we gain awareness of our inner polarities and oppositions, and follow the movements prompted by the Spirit. In "descending from the mind into the heart" through contemplative prayer and other spiritual practices, we are led to a greater awareness and deeper freedom, and are formed for a wider love for God and neighbor. This book on spiritual formation is based on his "theory" (if you can call it that) of dynamic *movements,* more like musical movements, in contrast to classical "stage theories," as the context of adult spiritual development. Though less systematic than other spiritual development conceptions, and limited to adult formation rather than over a lifetime, Nouwen's approach is organic and intuitive, insightful and compelling.

Two Journeys, Many Movements

The journey inward is the journey to find the Christ dwelling within us. The journey outward is the journey to find the Christ dwelling among us and in the world. The journey inward in communion requires the disciplines of solitude, silence, prayer, meditation, contemplation, and attentiveness to the movements of our heart. The journey outward in community and mission requires the disciplines of care, compassion, witness, outreach, healing, accountability, and attentiveness to the movement of other people's hearts. These two journeys belong together to strengthen each other, and should never be separated.[2]

Henri's theological reflection on the manifold journey of faith reveals that there are many transformative movements within each journey. Spiritual formation may begin with an inward journey to the heart, and then continue with an outward journey to community and ministry, then lead back to the inward journey.[3]

The heart, for Nouwen, is "that place where body, soul, and spirit come together as one." As the central unifying organ of our personal life, the heart is the "source of all physical, emotional, intellectual, volitional, and moral energies."[4] It is the seat of the will; it has intentions and makes choices. When we pray from the heart, we become familiar with the different complexities and polarities of our own inner life. When the heart is open and responsive to the Spirit within, we are ready to move from one state to another in relationship to ourselves, others, and God. For example, Nouwen writes in *Reaching Out*, one polarity deals with our relationship to ourselves—"the polarity between loneliness and solitude." A second polarity forms the basis of our relationship with others—"the polarity between hostility and hospitality." A third and most important polarity structures our relationship with God—"the polarity between illusion and prayer." These poles, he says, "offer the context in which we can speak about the spiritual life."

By reflecting on his own spiritual experience, and the experiences of others, Nouwen was able to articulate recognizable qualities and dynamics of the inner life in relation to spiritual formation. In his first book, *Intimacy: Essays in Pastoral Psychology*, he focused on the inner dynamics between fear, shame, vulnerability, identity, self-respect, anxiety, love, and hope. These psychological and spiritual polarities, he believed, prompt transformative movements—some major, others minor—within the spiritual journey. In the vacillation and dynamic tension, we are constantly moving back and forth in the spiritual life from *this* quality to *that*, from something enslaving and destructive to something liberating and life giving.

The journey motif implies that progress is possible, but not in a measurable upward way, with cumulative results. In cultures that value social progress, personal achievement, and human development, it is only natural that steps and standards are applied to spiritual development and formation. As Nouwen observes, one can be overly concerned and even consumed by questions such as: "How far have I advanced?"—"Have I matured since I started on the spiritual path?"—"On what level am I now, and how do I move to the next?"—"Am I in union with God?"—

"Have I experienced enlightenment yet?" Without dismissing the questions, Nouwen points in another direction. "Many great saints have described their religious experiences, and many lesser saints have systematized them into different phases, levels, or stages." These distinctions may be helpful for those who write books for instruction, "but it is of great importance that we leave the world of measurements behind when we speak about the life of the Spirit."[5]

PROGRESSIVE STAGES OR TRANSFORMATIVE MOVEMENTS?

The various movements of the spiritual life are not clearly separated, Nouwen observes, nor are they necessarily sequential. Yet, "certain themes recur in the different movements in various tonalities and often flow into one another as the different movements of a symphony."[6] In identifying the movements and polarities of our inner world, we can better recognize the dynamic elements of the spiritual life, discern the forces in our innermost self, and articulate how the Spirit of God is working in our life.

Nouwen came to this understanding of recurring movements at Notre Dame and continued to point out the pattern in books and lectures throughout his academic career at Yale and Harvard. For example, in one of this earliest books, *Pray to Live* (now titled *Thomas Merton: Contemplative Critic*), Nouwen identified the movements *from sarcasm to contemplation* and *from opaqueness to transparency*. In subsequent books, he identified other movements, usually in sets of three, each with a corresponding discipline: In *Reaching Out*, the first movement is *from loneliness to solitude*, requiring the discipline of silence; the second is *from hostility to hospitality*, inviting the discipline of ministry; the third movement is *from life's illusion to the prayer of the heart*, requiring both contemplative prayer and community discernment. In *Here and Now,* the movements include *from fatalism to faith, from worrying to prayer,* and *from mind to heart.* In *The Return of the Prodigal Son,* the movements are *from dissipation to homecoming, from resentment to gratitude,* and *from forgiven to forgiver.*

Only one movement stands out in some of his books: In *Creative Ministry,* there is the movement *from professionalism to creative ministry;* In *Making All Things New,* the movement *from alienation to community;* in *Compassion,* the movement *from competition to compassion;* in *The Inner Voice of Love,* the movement *from anguish to freedom;* in *With Burning Hearts,* the movement *from sorrow to joy.* In *Lifesigns,* the movement is *from the house of fear to the house of love.* And in *Our Greatest Gift,* the final movement in the human journey is *from aging to dying.* All told, twenty-six movements can be identified in the works of Nouwen, though seven seem to dominate.[7]

These movements of the Spirit may vary with the individual and with one's season of life and community of faith; yet no one's spiritual life is static, absolute, or perfectly completed, as if we must graduate from one movement to another before continuing our journey. Rather, we remain in motion and in the process of discerning which way the wind of God's activity is blowing in our life. The process involves becoming aware of and naming the subtle movements of Spirit. To live spiritually is to seek to breathe with the Spirit's rhythm and move in a God-ward direction on the long walk of faith.

CLASSICAL STAGE THEORY

As a Roman Catholic, Henri Nouwen inherited a rich tradition of spiritual disciplines and spiritual formation within the Catholic mystical tradition. Classical Christian spiritual development identifies three distinct stages of spiritual development— *purgation, illumination,* and *unification*—rooted in biblical reflection on the Exodus event as Israel was delivered from bondage to freedom with God.[8] Further reflection led many commentators to identify five distinct passages on the journey to God:

1. *awakening* (of desire);

2. *purgation* (of the passions);

3. *illumination* (of God);

4. *dark night* (of the soul); and

5. *unification* (with the Divine).[9]

In his early years as a priest who offered spiritual direction and supervision to seminarians and members of religious orders, Nouwen counseled others to follow the classical disciplines in order to climb the ladder of divine ascent in progressive stages of unification. Climbing Jacob's ladder, step by step, toward spiritual perfection is a common image and motif in classical stage theory. Nouwen had read John of the Ladder, the sixth-century ascetic who sought perfection in the desert, and Nouwen despaired of ever reaching the top.[10] By the time he arrived at Notre Dame as a professor of pastoral psychology, he had turned the ladder of ascent on its side and taught spiritual formation as a series of horizontal movements of the heart, back and forth, that require daily devotion and discipline, with the goal of human wholeness rather than divine perfection.

Nouwen had studied psychology and religion in seminary in Utrecht, Holland, graduated with a doctoral degree in psychology from Nijmegen University, and was trained in the new field of pastoral psychology at the Menninger Institute in Topeka, Kansas. He taught psychology at Notre Dame before teaching spirituality at Yale and Harvard. Nouwen often referred to himself as a "hyphenated priest" who used the classroom as his pulpit. As a priest-psychologist-professor, he was familiar with the relatively new field of depth psychology[11] and the many modern theories of psychosocial development. His education and keen self-reflection led him to apply his growing psychosocial understanding to classical spiritual teachings.

MODERN STAGE THEORIES

Like classical stage theory, modern stage theory posits structural norms of cognitive, moral, and faith development. Building on Jean Piaget's theory of cognitive development (1936), Erik Erikson's classic, *Childhood and Society*, laid out eight ages of the human life cycle (1950). These developmental roots informed subsequent stage theories of human development, including the work of Lawrence Kohlberg and Robert Kegan in the 1970s.

James Fowler's *Stages of Faith* (1981) was the first to apply stage theory to faith development over the human lifespan. Faith development, like emotional, cognitive, and moral development, according to Fowler, seems to have a broadly recognizable pattern of development.[12] Fowler's faith-development research finds itself among the branches of a tree of modern stage theories planted at Harvard University, where Erikson, Piaget, Kohlberg, Kegan, and Fowler all taught and conducted their research, and where Henri Nouwen later taught his notion of adult spiritual formation as transitional *movements*. Fowler's stage theory, nurtured by the theoretical roots of Erikson and Piaget, affirmed the trunk of Kohlberg's theory and bore good fruit in the form of the "six stages of faith."[13]

Fowler's structural conception of faith development has been critiqued and expanded over the years by other Harvard researchers, including Carol Gilligan and Sharon Parks, who provided the needed gender balance and challenge to male, majority cultural norms. Robert Kegan sought to integrate the various stage theories posited by Erikson, Piaget, Kohlberg, Fowler,

Gilligan, and Parks and stressed that life is *movement*—"the restless creative motion of life itself." What the other theorists called "stages" of development he calls "reference points of (temporary) stability" in the lifelong process of finding meaning in the world. These six "equilibrium stages" function as holding environments of transitional and transformative change.[14]

Henri Nouwen, though not consciously building on these earlier theories, nor trying to add another branch to the tree of developmental psychology, emerged at Notre Dame, continued at Yale, and ended his academic career at Harvard with a unique and profound perspective on what it means to be a spiritual person with powerful inner polarities and tensions, and how these contradictory forces prompt transformative movements in the journey of faith. The fruit of Nouwen's creative and integrative work in the field of pastoral psychology is a new, transformative, nonsystematic approach to spiritual formation. Some interpreters have called Nouwen's approach a "spirituality of imperfection."[15]

How Is Progress Possible?

If the movements are not necessarily sequential or progressive, if the inner polarities are never fully resolved, how is spiritual progress possible?

The movements of the Spirit, Nouwen observed within himself and in others, tend to come in cycles throughout our lives, with only a broad and hardly predictable progressive order. Instead of stepping up to higher and higher stages, as if achieving one stage leads to the next level and the next, we tend to vacillate back and forth between the poles that we seek to resolve. We move "from fear to love" and then back "from love to fear," for example, in a dynamic process that is never complete. Rather than resolving the tensions once and for all, the movements continue to call us to conversion and transformation. Rather than allowing us to conquer some aspect of life and move on to the next stage of spiritual development, we are called to return to prayer, to love, and to intimacy with God.

Over time, we may find the movement from resentment to gratitude, or from *this* quality to *that*, easier and more natural as we gain practice. As we "become more aware of the different poles between which our lives vacillate and are held in tension," Nouwen concludes, we can be more honest and speak more freely about the true realities of spiritual life. In the process, we gain greater awareness, personal freedom, and spiritual connection to God and others.[16]

CONCLUSION

Ultimately, for Nouwen, the spiritual journey is not to be found in the pursuit of perfection but in the practice of contemplative prayer leading to community and mission. Spiritual formation requires daily reflection and intentional practice. The process involves becoming aware, naming the condition, and following the subtle movements of the Spirit in our hearts and in our lives. Simply put, when the human heart is open and responsive to the Spirit, healthy movements occur and spiritual formation happens unexpectedly and in a variety of ways.

Notes

PREFACE

1. For Michael J. Christensen's treatment of how Nouwen's understanding of inner polarities and the dynamic nature of spiritual formation relates to stage theories in the history of faith development research, see the appendix.

2. For a list of twenty-six identified movements in Nouwen's works, see the appendix.

3. Each volume was developed by the editors in the aftermath of Nouwen's death to pull together the various strands of his teachings, unpublished and previously published, in the service of new contexts and readership.

4. Although the editors have used the term *visual divina* for many years in workshops and retreats, *visio divina*—the Latin version of *sacred seeing*—has started to appear on Web sites devoted to contemporary prayer and meditation.

   The postmodern practice of *visio divina*, combined with the ancient practice of *lectio divina*, provides an integrative, sensory, spiritual approach to connecting with divine creativity and presence in sacred word and image.

INTRODUCTION

1. Theophan the Recluse (1815–94) is a well-known saint in the Russian Orthodox tradition, credited with translating the *Philokalia* from Church Slavonic into Russian in the nineteenth century. He taught the practice of

continuous, interior prayer—or "praying without ceasing," as St. Paul admonished in his first letter to the Thessalonians. Nouwen's original source for Theophan's quotes is Timothy Ware, ed., *The Art of Prayer: An Orthodox Anthology* (Faber & Faber, 1966), p. 110. Quoted by Nouwen in *Reaching Out: The Three Movements of the Spiritual Life* (Doubleday, 1975) and in *The Way of the Heart: Desert Spirituality and Contemporary Ministry* (Seabury, 1981).

2. Thomas Hora, *Existential Meta-Psychiatry* (Seabury Press, 1977), quoted by Nouwen in "Spiritual Formation in Theological Education" and in *Clowning in Rome: Reflections on Solitude, Celibacy, Prayer, and Contemplation* (Doubleday, 1979).

3. Ware, *Art of Prayer*, p. 11.

4. *Mysterium tremendum* is a term coined by Rudolph Otto (1958) and used by Carl Jung and others to refer to the human encounter with the overwhelming nature of the inner life and its mysterious forces. *Mysterium* points to the otherness of the sacred; *tremendum*, to its overwhelming power within to shake one to the core. Cited by Nouwen simply as *inner tremendum* in "Generation Without Fathers," *Commonweal* 92:287–94 (June 1970); and in *The Wounded Healer: Ministry in Contemporary Society* (Doubleday, 1972), chap. 2.

5. Nouwen wrote this section in *The Wounded Healer* in 1972 (p. 132). His warnings seem rather prescient when read nearly forty years later.

6. Anton Boisen, *The Exploration of the Inner World* (Willett, Clark & Company, 1936), quoted by Nouwen in his article "Anton T. Boisen and Theology Through Living Human Documents," *Pastoral Psychology* 19 (September 1968): 49–63.

7. The maxim "what is most personal is most universal," which Nouwen used often, was also used by Anton Boisen and Carl Rogers.

8. *Lectio divina* can also apply to the devotional reading of other inspirational texts.

9. Sacred looking, or *visio divina*, is a contemporary term (not used by Nouwen) employed by the editors as a complementary practice to *lectio divina*, or sacred reading, following Nouwen's lead in *Behold the Beauty of the Lord: Praying with Icons* (Ave Maria Press, 1987).

10. For more on Nouwen's method of praying with icons and other images, see *Behold the Beauty of the Lord*.

11. Ware, *Art of Prayer*, p. 27.

CHAPTER ONE

1. Quoted by Nouwen in *Out of Solitude: Three Meditations on the Christian Life* (Ave Maria Press, 1974), p. 42.

2. According to Nouwen, Merton gave this teaching at a conference with the monks at Gethsemane Abbey. See *Clowning in Rome*, p. 89.

3. John Henry Newman, *Essays Critical and Historical*, vol. 2 (Longmans, Green, and Co., 1901), p. 192.

4. In the conclusion to *Clowning in Rome*, Nouwen goes on to describe *theologia* and the mystical doctrine of the "beatific vision" where theological distinctions disappear: "In this experience," for example, "the distinction between ministry and contemplation is no longer necessary, since here there are no more blindfolds to remove and all has become seeing" (p. 107).

5. *Clowning in Rome*, p. 94.

CHAPTER TWO

1. Quoted by Nouwen in *Out of Solitude*, p. 23. Adapted from "Tale of the Useless Tree" in *The Inner Chapters* by 4th century BCE Chinese philosopher Chuang Tzu.

2. The Hesychast tradition of interior prayer began with the Desert Fathers in the fourth century, developed in monasteries on Mount Sinai and Mount Athos, and continued in the *startsi* (holy ones) of nineteenth-century Russia; see R. M. French, trans., *The Way of a Pilgrim* (HarperCollins, 1965). The word *Hesychia* refers to the peace and repose of the soul when it is prayerfully anchored in God. *Hesychasm* is a method of praying with the heart without ceasing—a popular topic in Nouwen's courses on spiritual formation.

3. Quoted in Ware, *Art of Prayer*, p. 110; cited by Nouwen in *The Way of the Heart*.

4. See *The Way of the Heart* for Nouwen's extended reflection on this primary movement of the spiritual life.

5. Jean-Pierre de Caussade, *The Sacrament of the Present Moment* (Harper SanFrancisco, 1989), bk. 1, chap. 2, sec. 3. Caussade was a spiritual writer and an ordained member of the Society of Jesus. Henri Nouwen strongly recommended that all his students read Caussade's "little book on prayer."

6. *The Practice of the Presence of God* is a record of Brother Lawrence's conversations and letters as collected and published by Joseph de Beaufort, counsel to the archbishop of Paris, in 1691, the year that Brother Lawrence died.

7. In his courses at Yale and Harvard on spiritual formation, Nouwen often referred to the example of Brother Lawrence for how to "pray without ceasing" (1 Thess. 5:17).

8. *The Way of the Heart*, pp. 33–34.

9. Caussade, *Sacrament of the Present Moment*, bk. 1, chap. 2, sec. 1.

10. This section was compiled and edited from Nouwen's practical teachings on how to pray, primarily from "Prayer and Ministry: An Interview with Henri J. M. Nouwen," *Sisters Today* 48, no. 6 (February 1977): 345–55.

11. This section was compiled and edited from Nouwen's practical teachings on how to pray, primarily from the *Sisters Today* interview "Prayer and Ministry."

12. This section has been supplied by the editors.

CHAPTER THREE

1. Class handout (YDS, 1980). The full title of the handout is "A Tale from *The Teachings of the Compassionate Buddha*, E. A. Burtt, editor. New York: New American Library, 1955. P. 44ff." Nouwen used this story in his course of lectures on the topic of compassion at Yale Divinity School in 1980. The parable begins with this original introduction: "A tale is told of the Buddha, the Exalted One, the Possessor of the Ten Forces, and of how he taught his doctrines to the woman Kisa Gotami in the time of her overwhelming sorrow."

2. For an extended reflection about how Nouwen grieved the loss of his mother in relation to his father, see *A Letter of Consolation* (Harper & Row, 1982). For a similar reflection on grieving the loss of a close friendship, see *Spiritual Direction: Wisdom for the Long Walk of Faith* (HarperOne, 2006), chap. 8; and *The Inner Voice of Love: A Journey Through Anguish to Freedom* (Doubleday, 1996).

3. Daybreak is the name of the L'Arche community of people with disabilities near Toronto where Nouwen served as pastor from 1985 to 1996.

4. Luke 24:13–35.

5. A *lectio divina* exercise for Luke 24:13–35 is provided in the "Going Deeper" section later in this chapter.

6. For Nouwen's most polished reflection on the Eucharistic presence on the road to Emmaus, see *With Burning Hearts: A Meditation on the Eucharistic Life* (Orbis, 1994)

7. This meditation is adapted from "A Time to Mourn, A Time to Dance" (1977).

8. This section is gleaned from *Turn My Mourning into Dancing: Finding Hope in Hard Times* (W Publishing Group/Thomas Nelson, 2001), p. 15, and "Compassion: Solidarity, Consolation and Comfort," *America*, March 1976, p. 199.

9. This meditation on the sun in the paintings of Vincent van Gogh is an excerpt from "Compassion: Solidarity, Consolation and Comfort." Nouwen also taught a course at Yale Divinity School in 1979 called "The Ministry of Vincent van Gogh."

CHAPTER FOUR

1. "I don't know about you but this parable angers the hell out of me . . ." is what Nouwen said in class after reading the parable as an introduction to his lecture on resentment and gratitude. The version in this chapter is a blending of class notes (M. Christensen, Yale Divinity School lecture notes, 1979) and his reflection on the parable in *Home Tonight: Further Reflections on the Parable of the Prodigal Son* (Doubleday, 2009). See *Home Tonight*, p. 84.

2. Nouwen writes about his personal journey from resentment to gratitude in *The Return of the Prodigal Son* (Doubleday, 1992) and *Home Tonight;* see *Home Tonight*, pp. 85–88. In this chapter he reflects on resentment and gratitude in relation to theological education, spiritual formation, and ministry to the poor.

3. "Education to the priesthood" was the way Nouwen spoke of spiritual formation, and "real seminary education" is how he spoke of authentic Christian community in the context of the Roman Catholic Church in 1973. The editors updated and expanded these notions for this chapter.

4. *Turn My Mourning into Dancing*, p. 102.

CHAPTER FIVE

1. Similar versions of the text of this chapter appears in *Lifesigns: Intimacy, Fecundity, and Ecstasy in Christian Perspective* (Doubleday, 1986), p. 110, and in *The Road to Peace* (Orbis, 1998) pp. 56–57.

2. In *Gracias! A Latin American Journal* (Harper & Row, 1983) and *Love in a Fearful Land: A Guatemalan Story* (Orbis, 2006), Nouwen develops the theme of love and fear, and the gift of gratitude.

3. In *Peacework: Prayer Resistance Community* (Orbis, 2005), Nouwen develops the corporate practices that help us move from fear to love: prayer, resistance, and community. In *Lifesigns*, Nouwen says that the house of love has three main qualities: intimacy, fecundity, and ecstasy. These characteristics are the personal gifts and signs of those who live there together.

4. See *Lifesigns*, pp. 111–14, for Nouwen's vision of a global movement from fear to love through the practice of prayer, resistance, and community.

5. See *Peacework*, where one can find additional reflections and meditations by Nouwen on the theme of fear and love.

6. This section is adapted from "The Mystery of the Passion," from the video *From the House of Fear to the House of Love: A Spirituality of Peacemaking* (Center for Social Concerns, University of Notre Dame, 2002), and from *Behold the Beauty of the Lord*.

7. *Behold the Beauty of the Lord*, p. 20.

CHAPTER SIX

1. Benedicta Ward, trans., *The Sayings of the Desert Fathers* (Cistercian Publications, 1975); quoted by Nouwen in "The Monk and the Cripple: Toward a Spirituality of Ministry," *America* 142 (1980): 205–10.

2. The Community of the Ark—a community of people with physical and intellectual challenges in France and around the world. There is a community near Toronto, L'Arche Daybreak, at which Nouwen lived.

3. Nouwen has written in several places about his psychological breakdown soon after arriving at L'Arche—how his worldview was challenged, his

expectations shattered, and his emotional life torn apart. See *Spiritual Direction,* pp. 121–23.

4. Thomas Merton, private journal, March 19, 1958, published in *A Search for Solitude: Pursuing the Monk's True Life* (1996).

5. Thomas Merton, *Conjectures of a Guilty Bystander* (Doubleday, 1966), quoted by Nouwen in "Compassion: Solidarity, Consolation and Comfort."

6. Nouwen often used this familiar literary phrase, attributed to the Roman comic dramatist Terence (185–159 B.C.).

7. See Thomas Merton, *The Wisdom of the Desert: Sayings from the Desert Fathers of the Fourth Century* (Shambhala, 2004), p. 71.

8. The "mystery" Nouwen is trying to describe here is both the Roman Catholic doctrine of *transubstantiation* and the Eastern Orthodox teaching of *theosis.* Both concepts are ways of representing the mystical truth that when the Spirit of God takes up residence in human bodies, divinity becomes human, and humanity divine. In theological language, God becomes incarnate in Jesus, the first of many divine sons and daughters of God. And humanity, in the process of spiritual formation, is deified. For a full treatment of these theological concepts, see Michael J. Christensen and Jeffery Wittung, eds., *Partakers of the Divine Nature: Deification in the Christian Traditions* (Baker Academic, 2008).

9. This section is from Nouwen's article "Our Story, Our Wisdom," in *HIV/AIDS: The Second Decade,* ed. Robert Perelli and Toni Lynn Gallagher (National Catholic AIDS Network, 1995), p. 23; this article is a transcript of an address presented by Nouwen at the National Catholic AIDS Network Conference, Loyola University, Chicago, July 1995.

10. Gerhard Kittel and Gerhard Friedrich, eds., *Theological Dictionary of the New Testament,* 10 vols. (Eerdmans, 1964–74), provides three possibilities for the shape of the cross (*stauros*) of Christ: "The *stauros* is an instrument of torture for serious offenses. . . . In shape we find three basic forms. The cross was a vertical, pointed stake . . . or it consisted of an upright with a cross-beam above it . . . or it consisted of two intersecting beams of equal length" (7:572). The preference for the equal-armed cross within a circle is found in early Greek, Byzantine, and Celtic Christianity.

11. *Here and Now: Living in the Spirit* (Crossroad, 1995), p. 23.

12. This section is adapted from *Aging: The Fulfillment of Life* (Doubleday, 1974) and integrated with *Here and Now.*

13. R. M. Rilke, *Letters to a Young Poet* (Norton, 1963), cited in "Spirituality and the Family," *Weavings* 3, no. 1 (January–February 1988): 9.

CHAPTER SEVEN

1. *Our Greatest Gift,* p. 19.

2. *A Letter of Consolation,* p. 19.

3. Commonly attributed to German mystic Jakob Böhme (1575–1624), cited by Nouwen in "A Time to Mourn, a Time to Dance," p. 29.

4. James Hillman attended a seminar that Nouwen taught on Christian spirituality at Yale Divinity School in 1980, and he contributed to the discussion by introducing the concept of "befriending" those parts of ourselves and our reality that we often fear. See *A Letter of Consolation*, pp. 29–30.

5. Paul Monette wrote *Borrowed Time: An AIDS Memoir* (Harcourt Brace, 1988) after his partner died in 1986. Both are remembered for their activism in fighting homophobia and the stigma of AIDS.

6. For a full reflection on his "near-death experience," see *Finding My Way Home: Pathways to Life and the Spirit* (Crossroad, 2001) and *Beyond the Mirror: Reflections on Death and Life* (Crossroad, 1990).

7. This ancient Christian doctrine of imparted Christhood and divinity is known as *theosis*, or deification, in the Eastern Orthodox tradition. For further study, see Christensen and Wittung, *Partakers of the Divine Nature*.

8. The question of purgatory and praying for the dead was a major issue between Catholics and Protestants in the sixteenth century. The Council of Trent's 1563 decree about purgatory reaffirmed its existence and the usefulness of prayers for the deceased, yet it cautioned against curiosity and superstition. Today, the Roman Catholic teaching on purgatory reflects its understanding of the Communion of Saints—that we are connected to the saints in heaven, the saints-in-waiting in purgatory, and other believers here on earth. Prayers for the deceased are a means not of buying their way out of purgatory, but of believing in the "resurrection of the body and the life everlasting."

9. In "Befriending Death," his original address on this subject at the National Catholic AIDS Network Conference, Loyola University, Chicago, July 1995, Nouwen applied the doctrine of the Communion of Saints to the early AIDS crisis. He told his audience: "I think you and I are called to reclaim the incredible and beautiful choice of the community of saints. That means that people who have died before you and people who will die after you belong to one big family. You are just a small part of a much larger community that you have to grab and you have to feel. You belong to the people who went before you. You can talk about the saints of old like St. Francis or Benedict or Ignatius, and that is important, but because you have thousands of people who went before you, they are a new family. You have to hold onto them. You have to embrace them as saints. Yes, *those* who were born and died long ago struggled like you and I. They had their sexual struggles as I have, and they were lonely and depressed and confused. They went through the Black Plague. They, too, are a part of my human family. As far as I look back and as far as I look forward, I see this crowd of witnesses that I belong to. I am just there for a moment, but I have been there, and I will be there because of those who lived before and those who will

live after me. I think of the communion of saints as that incredible spiritual family that surrounds me and you and that makes our exodus from this life possible."

10. *A Cry for Mercy: Prayers from the Genesee* (Doubleday, 1981), March 24, p. 60.

11. Jakob Böhme's maxim is quoted in Henry Miller, *The Wisdom of the Heart* (New Directions, 1941), and is cited by Nouwen in *Turn My Mourning into Dancing*.

12. Henri's close friend Nathan Ball asked him this question after a community member died at Daybreak. The question, Nouwen said, "brought me face-to-face with a great challenge: not only how to live well, but also to die well." See the prologue to *Our Greatest Gift: A Meditation on Dying and Caring* (HarperCollins, 1994).

13. Joseph Cardinal Bernardin, *The Gift of Peace* (Loyola Press, 1997), pp. 127–28.

14. Matt. 17:1–8 (New Jerusalem Bible).

15. Fr. Rodney DeMartini, executive director of National Catholic AIDS Network, offered this meditation at the 1995 National Catholic AIDS Network Conference, which took place at Loyola University in Chicago July 20–25, 1995. There he introduced Henri Nouwen as the keynote speaker in this way: "To climb the mountain, to navigate its despair and its hope, its desolation and its vistas of glory, we need a guide, an experienced climber who knows when to ascend, when to cast off, when to hold tight, and when to let go. Henri Nouwen is such a guide. A priest of the Archdiocese of Utrecht, Holland, and renowned in North America for teaching at Notre Dame, Yale, and Harvard and for his numerous books which chart the life of the spirit. Psychologist, theologian, writer, and spiritual guide, Henri has been the pastor of the L'Arche Daybreak community in Ontario since 1986. From the L'Arche experience, he has helped us to realize that the world is not divided into the disabled and the able. We are more united than that. In a sense, we are all disabled, and in a profound sense, we are all able. Able human beings when it comes to loving and gathering together as community. Let us now welcome to the mound of this podium Henri Nouwen, who will guide us up the spirit mountain through shadows of desolation to the vista of seeing things in new light this great summer morning. Please help me welcome Henri Nouwen."

16. This section is adapted from "Compassion: Solidarity, Consolation and Comfort."

EPILOGUE

1. Elizabeth O'Connor, *Journey Inward, Journey Outward* (Harper & Row, 1968).

2. See Rebecca Laird, "How to Find a Spiritual Director," app. 2 of *Spiritual Direction*, by Henri J. M. Nouwen, ed. Michael J. Christensen and Rebecca Laird (HarperOne, 2006), pp. 155–60.

3. This volume, *Spiritual Formation*, on following the movements, is the second in an anticipated three-volume set on the introduction to the spiritual life by Henri Nouwen. The first volume, *Spiritual Direction*, on living the questions, was published in 2006. *Spiritual Discernment*, on reading the signs of daily life, is next. Each volume was developed by the editors in the aftermath of Nouwen's death to pull together the various strands of his teachings, both unpublished and previously published, in the service of new contexts and a new readership.

APPENDIX

1. *Reaching Out*, p. 10.

2. Course lecture notes and handout, "Communion, Community and Ministry: Introduction to the Spiritual Life" (YDS, 1980; Regis College, 1994); Nouwen draws on Elizabeth O'Connor, *Journey Inward, Journey Outward* (Harper & Row, 1978) for his journey motif.

3. "Communion, Community and Ministry."

4. See Nouwen's introduction to this book.

5. *Reaching Out*, p. 10.

6. *Reaching Out*, p. 12.

7. See the chapter titles in this book.

8. See Dionysius, *The Celestial Hierarchy*, chap. 3 and elsewhere.

9. See Gregory of Nyssa, *Life of Moses* and *From Glory to Glory,* and many other Patristic texts on perfection and the ascent to God.

10. John Climacus, *The Ladder of Divine Ascent*, cited by Nouwen in *Reaching Out*, p. 9.

11. *Depth psychology,* a broad term, refers to the exploration of the subtle movements and unconscious parts of human experience by bringing them into the light of consciousness. By uncovering, naming, and working with personal emotions, motives, dreams, complexes, motifs, and archetypes, healing and wholeness are possible. Though Nouwen would not identify himself as a depth psychologist, he seems to have been influenced by a number of depth psychologists, including Carl Jung, Anton Boisen, and James Hillman.

12. James W. Fowler, *Stages of Faith: The Psychology of Human Development and the Quest for Meaning* (HarperSanFrancisco, 1981). Fowler also summarized the emergence of the field of faith-development research thirty years after the publication of his first article on faith-development theory in his article "Faith Development at 30: Naming the Challenges of Faith in a New Millennium," *Religious Education* 99, no. 4 (Fall 2004).

13. According to Fowler, "our ways of imagining and committing to faith in faith correlate significantly with our ways of knowing and valuing more generally." Faith is more of a verb than a noun, he asserts. Faith is a meaning-making commitment to the Divine as well as a body of content and practices of particular faith traditions. "Faith orients one to life and its purposes, and to creation, with its origins, its ordering, its hospitality to life in its myriad forms and expressions, and its mystery." Further, faith-development theory suggests practical implications for ethics, theology, and spirituality. See Fowler, "Faith Development at 30."

14. Kegan, *The Emerging Self: Problem and Process in Human Development* (Harvard University Press, 1982). For a summary of Kegan's work in relation to that of his predecessors, see Joseph Powers, S. J., "Faith as Creative Assent," *Kerygma* 24 (1990): 193–207.

15. See Wil Hernandez, *Henri Nouwen: A Spirituality of Imperfection* (Paulist Press, 2006). For a similar approach to spiritual formation, see Richard Rohr's audio series *The Spirituality of Imperfection: Wisdom for the Second Half of Life* (St. Anthony Messenger Press, 2009).

16. *Reaching Out*, p. 10.

Primary Sources and Notations

Introduction: Spiritual Formation: The Way of the Heart

"Spiritual Formation in Theological Education" (Manuscript Series, 1970–79), Nouwen's unpublished manuscript on the subject, serves as the introduction to this book. It has been adapted and integrated with excerpts from *Reaching Out* (1975), pp. 10–11, 104; *The Wounded Healer* (1972), pp. 37–38; *The Way of the Heart* (1981), pp. 59–60, 76–77; and *Making All Things New* (1981), pp. 21–22.

Chapter One: From Opaqueness to Transparency

The core content of this chapter is adapted from "Prayer and Ministry: An Interview with Henri J. M. Nouwen," *Sisters Today* 48, no. 6 (February 1977): 345–55 (Manuscript Series—Collected Sermons and Lectures [1977–81]); and *Clowning in Rome* (1979) pp. 88–89, 94–101, 107. Additional excerpts are integrated from *Reaching Out* (1975), p. 104; and "Prayer and Health Care," a sound recording of Nouwen's address to the Seventy-fifth Annual Catholic Health Assembly in Washington, D.C., June 10–13, 1990.

The content of the *visio divina* reflection is supplied by editors based on Nouwen's comments in "Prayer and Ministry."

Chapter Two: From Illusion to Prayer

The core of this chapter is adapted from "Prayer and Health Care," pp. 27–48. Practical guidelines for prayer are from "Prayer and Ministry: An Interview with Henri J. M. Nouwen," *Sisters Today* 48, no. 6 (February 1977): 345–55 Additional content is supplied from *Out of Solitude* (1974) pp. 13–15, 20; *Here and Now* (1995), pp. 90–91; and *The Way of the Heart* (1981), p. 59.

The content for the *visio divina* is supplied by the editors, based on Nouwen's adaptation of the "Tale of the Useless Tree" by Chuang Tzu.

Chapter Three: From Sorrow to Joy

The content of this chapter is a consolidated text from many unpublished and previously published sources, including: "Prayer and Health Care" (1989–90), "Prayer and Ministry, An Interview with Henri J. M. Nouwen" (1977); "From Resentment to Gratitude" (speech to Grant McEwan Community College, sponsored by the Edmonton L'Arche Association, March 12, 1994); sermon notes on "The Road of Emmaus" from Luke 24, delivered at Yale Divinity School (1980); "A Time to Mourn, a Time to Dance" (address to Christian Counseling Services, Toronto, Ontario, February 4, 1992), pp. 15–16, subsequently published in part as the introduction and chapter 1 of *Turn My Mourning into Dancing* (Thomas Nelson Books, 1997) and in *Catholic New Times,* March 1992; *A Letter of Consolation* (1982), pp. 14–15; and *Letters to Marc About Jesus* (1988), p. 5. Additional excerpts are integrated from *With Burning Hearts* (1994), pp. 22, 31, 44, 46, 64.

The meditation on the movement from sorrow to joy is adapted from *A Time to Mourn, a Time to Dance* (1997), pp. 11–12, 16–17.

The content for the *visio divina* is gleaned and adapted from

"Compassion: Solidarity, Consolation and Comfort," *America*, March 13, 1976; and *Turn My Mourning into Dancing* (1992), p. 15.

Chapter Four: From Resentment to Gratitude

The content of this chapter is Nouwen's early unpublished 1973 lecture "From Resentment to Gratitude," presented to the National Conference of Catholic Seminarians in Chicago, April 28, 1973, and his later speech of the same title given at Grant McEwan Community College, sponsored by the Edmonton L'Arche Association, March 12, 1994. The editors added and integrated subsequent reflections and excerpts on the theme from "Turn My Mourning into Dancing" (manuscript, 1992); *Home Tonight* (2009), pp. 60–61, 81–82, 84–86; and *Gracias: A Latin American Journal* (1983), pp. 15–16, 18–19. The section "All Is Grace" was first polished and published in *Weavings*, November/December 1992. Nouwen's core sources and ideas are integrated and recontextualized here as the common human struggle to overcome the passion of resentment and move toward that attitude of gratitude in the church, community, family, and larger society.

Content for the *visio divina* reflection was supplied by the editors based on Nouwen's frequent comments in *Turn My Mourning into Dancing* (1992) about sculpting as a way of seeing and his imagined stonecutter creating a graceful dancer (p. 16).

Chapter Five: From Fear to Love

The primary sources for this chapter are consolidated adaptations and integrated excerpts from *From the House of Fear to the House of Love: A Spirituality of Peacemaking* (videotape, Center for Social Concerns, University of Notre Dame, 2002); "The Power of Love and the Power of Fear" (Presbyterian Peace Fellowship, 1985 published in *The Road to Peace*, pp. 56–57); "The Mystery of the Passion" (unpublished sermon, April 1984); *Lifesigns* (1986). pp. 15–16, 111–14, 120–21; *Peacework* (2005), p. 100; *Can You*

Drink the Cup (1996), pp. 74–75; *Our Greatest Gift* (1994) p. 17; and an interview at L'Arche Daybreak for University of Notre Dame (video recording, April 3, 1996, series 10, subseries 1, accession no. 2000 02).

The content for the *visio divina* reflection is from *Behold the Beauty of the Lord* (1987), pp. 19–24.

Chapter Six: From Exclusion to Inclusion

The core content of this chapter is adapted from Nouwen's article "Our Story, Our Wisdom," in *HIV/AIDS: The Second Decade*, ed. Robert J. Perelli and Toni Lynn Gallagher (National Catholic AIDS Network, 1995); this article is a transcript of an address presented by Nouwen at the National Catholic AIDS Network Conference at Loyola University, Chicago, July 26, 1994. The material is expanded and enhanced here by excerpts from "The Monk and the Cripple: Toward a Spirituality of Ministry, *America* 142 (1980): 205–10; "Compassion: Solidarity, Consolation and Comfort," *America*, March 13, 1976; "A Place Where God Wants to Dwell," *Compass* 7, no. 4 (1989): 34; "Spirituality and the Family," *Weavings* 3, no. 1 (1988); and *Reaching Out* (1975), p. 244.

The content for the *visio divina* is from "Our Story, Our Wisdom" (1995); *Here and Now* (1995), pp. 23–24.

Chapter Seven: From Denying to Befriending Death

The core of this chapter is "Befriending Death" (address to the National Catholic AIDS Network Conference, Loyola University, Chicago, July 1995 [unpublished manuscripts, 1995]), subsequently published in part in *Finding My Way Home* (2001). It is enhanced by excerpts from an unpublished sermon, "On Departure" (May 12, 1968), and from *Bread for the Journey* (1997), August 27. Additional excerpts are integrated from *Our Greatest Gift* (1982), pp. 11–19, and *A Letter of Consolation* (1982), pp. 29–30.

The meditation is from Joseph Cardinal Bernardin, *The Gift of Peace* (Loyola Press, 1997), pp. 127–28.

The *visio divina* content for reflection is adapted from Nouwen's article on Vincent van Gogh, "Compassion: Solidarity, Consolation and Comfort," *America*, March 13, 1976, and from descriptions supplied by the editors.

For Further Reading

Selected Books by Henri J. M. Nouwen

Aging: The Fulfillment of Life (Doubleday, 1974)

Behold the Beauty of the Lord: Praying with Icons (Ave Maria Press, 1987)

Bread for the Journey: A Daybook of Wisdom and Faith (HarperCollins, 1997)

Compassion: A Reflection on the Christian Life (Doubleday, 1982)

Here and Now: Living in the Spirit (Crossroad, 1995)

Home Tonight: Further Reflections on the Parable of the Prodigal Son (Doubleday, 2009)

In the Name of Jesus: Reflections on Christian Leadership (Crossroad, 1989)

Life of the Beloved: Spiritual Living in a Secular World (Crossroad, 1992)

Lifesigns: Intimacy, Fecundity, and Ecstasy in Christian Perspective (Doubleday, 1986)

Making All Things New: An Invitation to the Spiritual Life (HarperCollins, 1981)

Our Greatest Gift: A Meditation on Dying and Caring (HarperCollins, 1994)

Reaching Out: The Three Movements of the Spiritual Life (Doubleday, 1975)

The Inner Voice of Love: A Journey Through Anguish to Freedom (Doubleday, 1996)

The Return of the Prodigal Son (Doubleday, 1992)

The Selfless Way of Christ: Downward Mobility and the Spiritual Life (Orbis, 2007)

The Way of the Heart: Desert Spirituality and Contemporary Ministry (Seabury, 1981)

The Wounded Healer: Ministry in Contemporary Society (Doubleday, 1972)

Thomas Merton: Contemplative Critic (Harper & Row, 1972)

With Burning Hearts: A Meditation on the Eucharistic Life (Orbis, 1994)

Selected Compilations and Edited Volumes by and About Henri J. M. Nouwen

Bengtson, Jonathan, and Gabrielle Earnshaw, eds., *Turning the Wheel: Henri Nouwen and Our Search for God* (Orbis, 2007)

Greer, Wendy Wilson, ed. and comp., *The Only Necessary Thing: Living a Prayerful Life: Selected Writings of Henri J. M. Nouwen* (Crossroad, 1999)

Hernandez, Wil, *Henri Nouwen: A Spirituality of Imperfection* (Paulist Press, 2006)

Jonas, Robert A., ed., *The Essential Henri Nouwen* (Shambhala, 2009)

Laird, Rebecca, and Michael J. Christensen, eds., *The Heart of Henri Nouwen: His Words of Blessing* (Crossroad, 2003)

LaNoue, Deirdre, *The Spiritual Legacy of Henri Nouwen* (Continuum, 2000)

Mosteller, Sue, ed., *Finding My Way Home: Pathways to Life and the Spirit* (Crossroad, 2001)

Nouwen, Henri J. M., *Spiritual Direction: Following the Movements of the Spirit,* ed. Michael J. Christensen and Rebecca Laird (HarperOne, 2006)

———, *Turn My Mourning into Dancing: Finding Hope in Hard Times,* ed. Timothy Jones (W Publishing Group/Thomas Nelson, 2001)

O'Rourke, Michelle, *Befriending Death: Henri Nouwen and the Spirituality of Dying* (Orbis, 2009)

Classical Texts

Anonymous, *The Way of a Pilgrim*, trans. Helen Bacovcin (Image, 1978)

Athanasius, *The Life of St. Anthony*, trans. Robert Meyer, *Ancient Christian Writers*, vol. 10 (Newman Press, 1978)

Augustine of Hippo, *The Confessions of St. Augustine*, trans. Rex Warner (New American Library, 1963)

Bernard of Clairvaux, *The Love of God*, ed. James Houston (Multnomah, 1983)

Bonhoeffer, Deitrich, *The Cost of Discipleship* (Macmillan, 1978)

———, *Life Together* (Harper & Row, 1954)

Caussade, Jean-Pierre de, *The Sacrament of the Present Moment* (HarperSanFrancisco, 1989)

Chariton of Valamo, Igumen, comp., *The Art of Prayer: An Orthodox Anthology* (Faber and Faber, 1966)

Climacus, John, *The Ladder of Divine Ascent* (Paulist, 1982)

Dionyisus, *The Celestial Hierarchy* (Paulist, 1987)

Doherty, Catherine de Haeck, *Poustinea: Christian Spirituality of the East for Western Man* (Ave Maria Press, 1983)

Eckhart, Meister, *Treatises on the Love of God* (Harper & Row, 1968)

St. Francis de Sales, *Introduction to the Devout Life*, trans. John Ryan (Doubleday, 1955)

Gregory of Nyssa, *Life of Moses* and *From Glory to Glory*, in *The Classics of Western Spirituality*, trans. Abraham Malherbe and Everett Ferguson (Paulist, 1987)

Guyon, Madame, *Experiencing the Depths of Jesus Christ* (Christian Books, 1975)

St. Ignatius of Loyola, *The Spiritual Exercises of St. Ignatius*, trans. Anthony Mottola (Doubleday, 1964)

St. John of the Cross, *The Ascent of Mount Carmel* (Paraclete Press, 2002)

———, *Dark Night of the Soul*, trans. Mirabai Starr (Riverhead, 2003)

Johnston, William, *The Mysticism of the Cloud of Unknowing*, with a foreword by Thomas Merton (Desclee, 1967)

Llewelyn, Robert, ed. *Enfolded in Love: Daily Readings with Julian of Norwich* (Darton, Longman, and Todd, 2004)

———, *The Revelations of Divine Love*, trans. Elizabeth Spearing, with an introduction and notes by A. C. Spearing (Penguin, 1999)

Kadloubovsky, E., trans., *Early Fathers from the Philokalia* (Faber and Faber, 1954)

Kadloubovsky, E., and G. E. H. Palmer, trans., *Writings from the Philokalia: On Prayer of the Heart* (Faber and Faber, 1992)

Kelly, Thomas, *A Testament of Devotion* (Harper & Row, 1941)

Br. Lawrence, *The Practice of the Presence of God* (Revell, 1958)

Merton, Thomas, *Conjectures of a Guilty Bystander* (Doubleday, 1966)

———, *Contemplation in a World of Action* (Doubleday, 1971)

———, *Contemplative Prayer* (Herder and Herder, 1969)

———, *The Seven Storey Mountain* (Harcourt Brace, 1948)

———, ed., *The Wisdom of the Desert: Sayings from the Desert Fathers of the Fourth Century* (Shambhala, 2004)

Mottola, Anthony, trans., *The Spiritual Exercises of St. Ignatius* (Doubleday, 1964)

Teresa of Ávila, *The Interior Castle* (Image, 1972)

———, *The Way of Perfection* (Image, 1991)

St. Thérèse of Lisieux, *The Story of a Soul*, trans. John Beevers (Image, 1989)

Ward, Benedicta, trans., *The Sayings of the Desert Fathers* (Mowbray & Co., 1975)

Ware, Kallilstos, *The Orthodox Way* (St. Vladimir's Seminary Press, 1995)

Ware, Timothy, ed., *The Art of Prayer: An Orthodox Anthology* (Faber & Faber, 1966)

Contemporary Texts

Barton, Ruth Haley, *Sacred Rhythms: Arranging our Lives for Spiritual Transformation* (InterVarsity, 2006)

Bernardin, Cardinal Joseph, *The Gift of Peace* (Image, 1998)

Bloom, Anthony, *Beginning to Pray* (Paulist, 1970)

Christensen, Michael J., and Jeffery A. Wittung, *Partakers of the Divine Nature: The History and Development of Deification in the Christian Traditions* (Baker Academic, 2007)

Forest, Jim, *Road to Emmaus: Pilgrimage as a Way of Life* (Orbis, 2007)

Foster, Richard, *Celebration of Discipline: The Path to Spiritual Growth* (HarperSanFrancisco, 1978)

Foster, Richard J., *Prayer: Finding the Heart's True Home* (HarperSanFrancisco, 1992)

Fowler, James, *Stages of Faith* (Harper & Row, 1981)

Holmes, Barbara A., *Joy Unspeakable: Contemplative Practices of the Black Church* (Fortress, 2004)

Kegan, Robert, *The Evolving Self: Problem and Process in Human Development* (Harvard University Press, 1982)

Lewis, C. S., *Letters to Malcolm: Chiefly on Prayer* (Harcourt, Brace & World, 1964)

———, *Surprised by Joy* (Harcourt, Brace, 1956)

Mulholland, M. Robert, *Invitation to a Journey: A Road Map for Spiritual Formation* (InterVarsity, 1993)

Muto, Susan, *Pathways of Spiritual Living* (Epiphany Books, 2004)

O'Connor, Elizabeth, *Journey Inward, Journey Outward* (Harper & Row, 1968)

Peterson, Eugene, *The Contemplative Pastor* (Word, 1989)

Rohr, Richard, *The Spirituality of Imperfection: Wisdom for the Second Half of Life* (audio recording) (St. Anthony Messenger Press, 2009)

Solle, Dorothie, *Mysticism and Resistance* (Fortress, 2001)

Steindl-Rast, Brother David, *Gratefulness, the Heart of Prayer: An Approach to Life in Fullness* (Paulist, 1984)

Thomson, Marjorie J., *Soul Feast: An Invitation to the Christian Life* (Westminster John Knox, 1995)

Vanier, John, *Be Not Afraid* (Paulist, 1975)

———, *Community and Growth* (Paulist Press, 1979)

———, *Essential Writings* (Orbis, 2008)

Willard, Dallas, *Renovation of the Heart: Putting on the Character of Christ* (Now Press, 2002)

———, *The Spirit of the Disciplines* (Harper Collins, 1988)

Credits

ART CREDITS

Figure 1: Theophan the Greek (c.1330-1410). *Transfiguration from Pereslavl.* Russian Icon. c. 1403. Reprinted by permission of: Scala / Art Resource, NY. Tretyakov Gallery, Moscow, Russia

Figure 2: Gogh, Vincent van (1853-1890). *The Bench at Saint-Remy,* 1889. Canvas. Reprinted by permission of: Erich Lessing / Art Resource, NY. Museu de Arte, Sao Paulo, Brazil

Figure 3: Gogh, Vincent van (1853-1890). *Sunflowers,* 1889. Oil on canvas, 95 x 73 cm. Inv. F 458. Reprinted by permission of: Art Resource, NY. Van Gogh Museum, Amsterdam, The Netherlands

Figure 4: Canova, Antonio (1757-1822). *Woman Dancing.* 1809-1812. Marble statue, h. (without base) 187 cm. Inv. 2/81. Photo: Antje Voigt. Reprinted by permission of: Bildarchiv Preussischer Kulturbesitz / Art Resource, NY. Skulpturensammlung und Museum fuer Byzantinische Kunst, Staatliche Museen, Berlin, Germany

Figure 5: Rublev, Andrei (1360-c.1430). *Icon of the Old Testament Trinity,* c.1410. Reprinted by permission of: Scala / Art Resource, NY. Tretyakov Gallery, Moscow, Russia

Figure 6: Apse mosaic: *Allegory of Transfiguration* (with Saint Apollinaris). Early Christian. Reprinted by permission of: Scala / Art Resource, NY. S. Apollinare in Classe, Ravenna, Italy

Figure 7: Artwork by Francis Maurice, Tracy Westerby, and Amanda Wittington-Ingram, members of L'Arche Daybreak in Richmond Hill, Ontario, Canada.

Figure 8: Gogh, Vincent van (1853-1890). *Old Man with His Head in His Hands.* Reprinted by permission of: Francis G. Mayer/CORBIS